teach
yourself ®

wine
tasting
godfrey spence

The **teach yourself** series does
exactly what it says, and it works.
For over 60 years, more than
40 million people have learnt over
750 subjects the **teach yourself**
way, with impressive results.

be where you want to be
with **teach yourself**

To Allison Elaine Spence and Elspeth Corilin, both of whom are in part responsible for my interest in food, and therefore taste.

For UK orders: please contact Bookpoint Ltd., 130 Milton Park, Abingdon, Oxon OX14 4SB. Telephone: (44) 01235 827720. Fax: (44) 01235 400454. Lines are open from 09.00–18.00, Monday to Saturday, with a 24-hour message answering service. You can also order through our website www.madaboutbooks.co.uk

For U.S.A. order enquiries: please contact McGraw-Hill Customer Services, P.O. Box 545, Blacklick, OH 43004-0545, U.S.A. Telephone: 1-800-722-4726. Fax: 1-614-755-5645.

For Canada order enquiries: please contact McGraw-Hill Ryerson Ltd., 300 Water St, Whitby, Ontario L1N 9B6, Canada. Telephone: 905 430 5000. Fax: 905 430 5020.

Long renowned as the authoritative source for self-guided learning – with more than 30 million copies sold worldwide – the *Teach Yourself* series includes over 300 titles in the fields of languages, crafts, hobbies, business and education.

British Library Cataloguing in Publication Data
A catalogue record for this title is available from The British Library

Library of Congress Catalog Card Number: On file

First published in UK 2003 by Hodder Headline Plc, 338 Euston Road, London, NW1 3BH.

First published in US 2003 by Contemporary Books, A Division of The McGraw-Hill Companies, 1 Prudential Plaza, 130 East Randolph Street, Chicago, Illinois 60601 U.S.A.

The 'Teach Yourself' name and logo are registered trade marks of Hodder & Stoughton Ltd.

Copyright © 2003 Godfrey Spence

Cover photo from Graham Ford/Getty Images
Photographs on pages 2, 5, 8, 9 from Mick Rock/CEPHAS
Typeset by Dorchester Typesetting Group Ltd
Printed in Great Britain for Hodder & Stoughton Educational, a division of Hodder Headline Plc, 338 Euston Road, London NW1 3BH by Cox & Wyman Ltd., Reading, Berkshire.

Impression number   10 9 8 7 6 5 4 3 2 1

Year   2009 2008 2007 2006 2005 2004 2003

contents

v

In the past 30 years the consumption of wine in countries outside the traditional European producing nations, and in the UK in particular, has grown beyond the wildest dreams of most producers. At the same time consumption in the main wine-producing countries has declined dramatically, but the value of each litre has increased. So we are now drinking better wines than ever before.

The wine trade once simply peddled famous names from a handful of classic sites in three or four countries to the *cognoscenti*, and big name brands to the rest of us. Names such as Don Cortez, Hirondelle and Cloberg offered security to beginner or occasional wine drinkers who felt intimidated by the arcane mysteries of the appellations seen on the finer wines, while those who could afford them tucked into their Mersaults and Margaux, with precious little in between. But the wine world has changed. Customers know more about wine, and cannot now be fobbed off with dreary, sub-standard drinks, with or without a famous brand name and consumer demand has led to far greater availability of well-made, medium-priced wines.

Retailers have come to terms with the modern customer who demands wine made in a modern fashion where the flavour of the grape, and very often the flavour of oak, are all-important. Clean, up-front, fruity styles of wine dominate the market, but significantly it is the style that matters. Provenance has become secondary. To some extent this has led to a 'sameness' in certain parts of the market. Inexpensive oaked Chardonnay is made in almost any wine-producing country, and will taste pretty similar whichever you choose. But regional differences and traditions do still exist; Bordeaux is still different from Burgundy, Chianti or Barossa.

For the knowledgeable consumer this is like having Christmas every day. The general standard of wines is getting better, while the price of most wines is, in real terms, falling through increased competition. But where does it leave the beginner? Most wine is now bought from supermarkets, where advice is usually unobtainable and where the plethora of different labels is most confusing. The shopper is confronted with a wall of bottles, dozens of Chardonnays, Cabernets and Merlots, let alone the rest, many at similar prices, with similar names. Where does one start?

This book will help you navigate those shelves. Each major style of wine is looked at and explained, both from a production viewpoint (how did Wine 'X' end up tasting the way it did?) and from a usage point of view – what food will go with this wine, and why? Perhaps most importantly, this book aims to be a practical way of learning about wine. Within each chapter there are exercises in tasting, with guidance notes to explain the differences and similarities between wines. By following these you will widen your tasting experience and understand more fully what the marketing blurb on the labels really means.

With greater knowledge and understanding of the liquid inside the bottle, you will gain more confidence to select from that ever-increasing range in the supermarket or off-licence, and you will be able to avoid the pitfalls of a wrong choice. Moreover, by practising tasting, rather than just drinking, you will find you enjoy each glass more, and therefore get better value for money from it.

the mechanics of tasting

Tasting is educational, it tells you a lot about the wine, and it can be great fun. Many people join tasting groups or go along to ad hoc social tastings for that very reason, but accurate and precise tasting does require discipline, concentration and the use of at least four senses: sight, smell, taste and touch. Sound can also be important. It can affect your judgement in both positive and negative ways. The 'pop' of a cork or the chink of glasses puts us in a positive frame of mind, eagerly anticipating the taste to follow. More seriously, it is all too easy to be misled by other people's comments on wine, which is why judging at the better wine competitions is silent. A producer telling you about the qualities of his or her wine as you taste it will inevitably cloud your judgement, and the wine may not taste nearly as good on other occasions. Conversely, the merest whisper of a wine fault in a room, even of experienced tasters, can convince others present that their glass is also at fault. It is important in wine tasting to be honest with yourself; do not take someone else's word when he or she says a particular wine is the best (or worst) in the world. Try it critically yourself and come to your own decision.

Appearance

The way a wine looks can tell you a great deal about it. In order to assess the wine accurately you will need a clear glass, ideally the ISO (see Chapter 14), and good natural light. One of the reasons trade tastings take place in the morning is the availability of natural light, something that cannot be guaranteed late on a winter's afternoon. A clean white surface helps too, a white tablecloth is perfect, while being a neutral colour will not affect your assessment of the wine's hue.

The first consideration is the health of the wine. It should look appealing, be clear and bright, and generally free from effervescence. A little sediment in old red wines or tartrate crystals in fine wines are nothing to worry about, but if the wine is cloudy there may be a fault. Similarly with bubbles. A few lazy bubbles round the edge of the wine or clinging to the base of the glass are probably just a sign of good cellar practice – bottling without too much disturbance, or bottling under a protective blanket of carbon dioxide to avoid oxidation – but if the wine is fizzy when it is meant to be still there may be a secondary fermentation taking place (see pages 57–8).

Secondary fermentation is a fault that rarely occurs these days, but is an ever-present hazard in medium sweet wines. Residual sugar in the wine makes it inherently unstable and any active yeast or bacteria that successfully navigates the filtration regime will cause an unwanted fermentation, resulting in fizzing and an odd smell and taste of yeast in the wine.

Looking at a glass of wine side-on does not tell you very much about the content – as you will see in the red wine exercise – and the uncomfortable stance taken by many beginners trying to look through the wine from below is more likely to lead to a cricked neck or wine spilt in the eye than to any meaningful increase in knowledge about the wine. Try this with two different red wines, one

to assess the appearance of a wine, look at it with a white surface behind it – a white table cloth, or just a piece of white paper will do you are looking for clarity, and at the colour

young and one older, a basic vin de pays red, the youngest you can get hold of, and a Reserva Rioja would be ideal. With a tasting sample in each glass look at the glasses side on. There will be some difference in colour, but not much. Now, hold the glass at an angle of between 30 and 45 degrees and look down on the wine, preferably over a white surface so you get an accurate idea of the colour. Holding the glass in this way forms a wedge of wine in the glass, which, because of the varying thickness, gives a range of colours. In this case you will rapidly see how the older wine is far browner, particularly at the narrowest point, the rim of the wine.

White wines tend to deepen in colour with age, but certain grapes and wine-making techniques give deeper colours so this is not always a sign of age.

Red wines start off purple in colour and get paler with age, at the same time losing this colour and taking on first a ruby appearance, then turning to brick-red and eventually tawny or brown. This is because the anthocyanin compounds in the grape skin change their chemical composition over time.

white wines tend to deepen with age – eventually turning brown

red wines lighten with age and the colour changes from purple red through ruby to brick-red, tawny and eventually brown

Again, grape variety and vinification play their part so you cannot necessarily say one wine is older than another just from the hue – it is easy to find a pair of red wines, even from the same region, that are the same vintage but very different colours.

In white wines, it is really just the colour and its depth that are worth noting – the colour usually fades towards the rim. With red wines, there often seem to be two colours exhibited, one in the core of the glass and a paler one on the rim. This is why tasters will usually hold their glass at an odd angle away from themselves when tasting, and why white tablecloths and neutral light are *de rigueur* for serious tasting sessions.

You will often hear tasters referring to a wine's 'legs' – sometimes called tears or even, rather poetically, cathedral windows. These form when you swirl the wine around the glass and allow it to settle. These only indicate a high alcohol or sweetness. Their presence or absence is not an indication of quality.

legs, or tears, forming on the sides of a glass – they only indicate alcohol

The nose

Most people think we taste with our mouths, but in fact, the mouth, or palate, is a very poor organ to taste with. Most of our sensations of taste come from our sense of smell, not from the palate. Think about how dull food seems when you have a bad cold – the reason is simply that you cannot smell it. To prove this, you can do a very simple exercise. You will need a friend to assist.

Arrange for a friend else to take a few drops of vanilla essence and put them in a tasting glass with about 50 ml water. The friend should also put a similar amount of water in two other identical glasses. Hold your nose firmly so you cannot smell anything, taste each in turn, and try to decide which of the three contains the essence. Even with an easy-to-recognize taste like vanilla, it will be impossible. Now release your nose and try again. This time it will be ridiculously easy, the flavour coming through very clearly only when you can smell it.

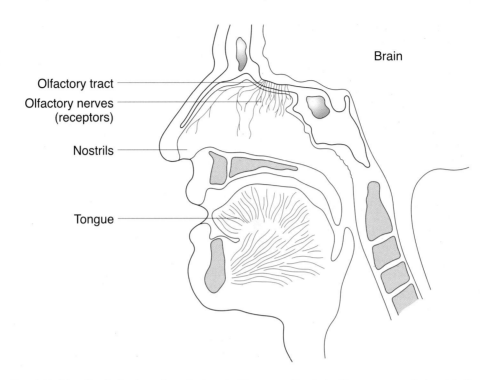

Brain

Olfactory tract

Olfactory nerves
(receptors)

Nostrils

Tongue

the nasal cavity – taste is really all about smell, we taste not with our mouths, but with our noses – fortunately the nasel cavity connects to our mouth

The nose is an amazing organ. We can all smell an infinite number of different smells, each of which is a different chemical compound or combination of compounds. Most of what we 'taste' we actually smell. The difference between rosemary and basil, between raspberry and mint or chocolate and liquorice is not the taste in the mouth but the smell, either before or after we put it into our mouths. It is very rare to find anyone who cannot smell – far rarer than people who cannot see or hear – but to identify smells needs practice. Many people doing the experiment above blind would know the smell, but be unable to identify it.

We do, however, all have 'blind spots' in smells. About 10 per cent of the population will be 'blind' to any particular pure smell; a function of anosmia – or smell blindness. Fortunately, the flavour of wine is made up of hundreds of different components, so there will always be something to enjoy. We are also blind to certain tastes, for example a significant proportion of the population cannot taste the bitterness of quinine in tonic water. There is nothing that can be done about it, it is just one of those things.

The smell of wine, as with the smell of anything else, comes to us in two ways. First, physically and deliberately smelling the glass, and second through retro-olfaction – experiencing smells via the back of the mouth when the vapour from the wine in our mouths reaches the nasal cavity via the back of the mouth. We will look further at this phenomenon when we look more closely at the palate.

Smelling wine

When tasting a wine it is always good practice to give the glass a good sniff before you start – at trade tastings the first thing the tasters do is smell their empty glasses, often to the amusement of the waiting staff at the venue. This is the wine trade equivalent of a chef checking the edge of the knives, or a photographer checking the cleanliness of the lens. A dirty glass, or one that smells of the cardboard box in which it has been kept, or last night's washing-up detergent, will not be a useful tool.

Remember to fill the glass only to about one-third full. Once the wine is in the glass, having another quick sniff before you swirl it around is always a good idea. Occasionally you will come across a nasty wine fault that is so pungent that anything more vigorous could give your nose a nasty shock. This is particularly important if you ever taste wine from a tank in the producer's cellar – a recently sulphured wine (one where the wine maker has just added more sulphur dioxide) can knock out your taste buds for quite a while.

Assuming all is fine, swirl the wine around the glass, allowing it to get as far up the sides of the glass as possible. (One of the reasons professional tasters prefer the ISO glass is the shape – the wine rarely spills over!) This will increase the surface area, allowing more of the volatile components – those that we can smell – to be released through evaporation. Then put your nose into the glass and take a gentle but long and deep sniff. The first thing that you will notice is how much more pronounced the wine smells this time than before you swirled it around.

after an initial gentle sniff, put your nose as far into the glass as possible and give the wine a deep but gentle sniff

There are three things you should be looking for on the nose: cleanliness, intensity of character and the character itself. With experience you will also be able to identify the development of any given glass; for example does it smell youthful or developed?

The first, cleanliness, is an initial reaction. Identification of specific wine faults is a skill that can come only with practice, but knowing whether the wine smells clean and appealing is automatic. Humans are pre-programmed to recognise bad smells, a self-defence mechanism that has developed during evolution so our cave-dwelling ancestors could avoid rotten food and the poisoning that went with it. No common wine fault is likely to cause serious health problems but you won't want to take the tasting much further if the wine smells faulty. We will look at wine faults, how they occur and how to identify them in Chapter 13.

Next is intensity. As we will see in later chapters, some wines are aromatic and even quite pungent, while others make a positive virtue out of their neutrality. This is not

swirling the wine increases the surface area and releases the flavour components

a qualitative assessment of the wine but a descriptive one. More aromatic wines, being easier to smell, are of course easier to describe too, but that does not necessarily make them better wines. We will look at the intensity of fruit or other flavours on the palate too.

Some wines, such as Sauvignon and Gewürztraminer, have a strongly aromatic character that leaps out of the glass to greet you. Others, such as Muscadet, Soave and Frascati are far weaker on the nose.

Allied to the fruit character is the development. Recognizing development takes a little practice and experience, and is closely tied into the specific characteristic you smell in the wine. Wine is said to have three separate ranges of smell: the primary aromas are those derived from the grape itself, the secondary from the fermentation process and tertiary from the subsequent maturation.

Young wines have a vibrant, fruity flavour. It can be simple or complex, but it is a smell of primary fruit. Development implies greater complexity, with layers of, perhaps, spice, leather or chocolate.

When very young, wine smells of the fermentation. We normally do not get to experience this unless we are visiting a winery, but wines such as Beaujolais Nouveau, if tasted on the release date, can have something of this left. After a short time this disappears and the youthful fruit aromas come to the fore. Later, through cask or bottle maturation, the nose changes and becomes more developed, and eventually aged. Smells that indicate development include spice, tobacco, cigar boxes, chocolate and earthiness. Not all wines are meant to develop these tertiary aromas, most are meant to be consumed when released, or shortly after. By convention the fruit and fermentation smells are referred to as aroma, whereas the maturation character is called bouquet.

Identification and description

It is remarkably difficult to identify exact smells when you begin to taste, and seeing professionals either on television or in print listing a whole fruit basket of flavours in a wine that you think simply smells of wine can be terribly off-putting for the beginner. Do not be alarmed. Practice will improve your ability to separate out the various components of the smell. Furthermore, there is a big difference between tasting wine for your own pleasure and education, and wine tasting for public consumption, which must have entertainment value – a page from a professional wine-tasting record in a blender's cellar would not sell newspapers, far less make it to primetime television.

The exact descriptions of wine are a difficult subject. In beer tasting the professionals are mostly tasting as part of quality control and so there is an internationally agreed set of very specific flavours and tastes that they are looking for. There is also an agreed set of terminology, most of which is based on the chemical formulas, or production techniques that are used to identify faults or particular characters that brewers and consumers value.

In wine descriptions we are far less restricted. Wine is described either as a sales aid or as an *aide-mémoire* for the individual enthusiast. It is therefore of the utmost importance that the description is of use to the person for whom it is intended. Chemical names are not widely understood so common, everyday terms such as fruity and spicy take their place. You will find that wine will remind you of all sorts of strange things – fruit, spice, vegetable, earth, oil, wax, sawdust or almost anything else. When you are writing notes for your own use, use whatever is meaningful to you.

There are many instances of one country's 'standard' tasting notes being of no use in another. English wine literature often describes classic Sauvignon Blanc as being like gooseberry. American wine writers have borrowed this term, yet the tart, acidic English gooseberry is almost unknown in the USA. To South African wine makers gooseberry means the sweet, orange berry that grows in a paper-like lantern of leaves, the Cape gooseberry, or physalis; a very different fruit. Some fruit goes by different names in different places, so what is a granadilla in South Africa is a passion fruit in Britain. Other fruit is not available in some markets. Markets in the Far East are full of all manner of exotic fruit and vegetables simply not seen in the West, but equally the shopper in Tokyo or Singapore may have never seen juniper berries, Cox's apples or quinces. Looking back at older wine books, even those written in the 1970s and 1980s, is instructive too. Alsace Gewürztraminer was always described then as spicy – logical giving the origins of the name – but never as tasting of lychee, today's standard descriptor. Lychees were hardly known in Britain at the time.

Flavour characters

Some typical characters found in some of the most widely used grapes include:

Chardonnay	Riesling	Muscat	Sauvignon Blanc	Sémillon
banana	apricot	apricot	asparagus	fat
butter	aromatic	aromatic	blackcurrant leaves	oil
butterscotch	floral	bath salts	catty	rich
citrus	kerosene	grape	flinty	toast
creamy	lemon	peaches	floral	tropical fruit
green apple	lime	perfumed	gooseberry	waxy
lime	mineral	soap	grass	
nuts	oil		green apple	
pineapple	petrol		green fruit	
timber yard	rose petal		nettles	
toasty	sealing wax		tinned peas	
tropical fruit	slatey		tom cat's pee	
vanilla	steely			
wood				

Viognier	Pinot Noir	Cabernet Sauvignon	Syrah/Shiraz	Merlot
apricot	cabbage	blackberry	animalesque	cherries
ginger	compost heap	blackcurrant	blackcurrant	damson
peach	ethereal	black pepper	dark fruit	dark fruit
spice	farmyard	cassis	earthy	plum
	horse manure	cedar	hot fruit	red fruit
	raspberry	cigar box	jam	rich
	summer pudding	green (bell) pepper	leather	soft
	tinned strawberry	leather	medicinal	
	vegetal	mint	oak	
	violets	oak	spice	
		plums		
		prunes		
		Ribena		
		tea leaves		
		tobacco		

Of course, if you are planning to publish your notes, or are preparing for an international examination in wine, you will have to use terms to which others can relate. In this book the terms will generally be those that are in normal use in the British wine trade.

What we are smelling in wine is a vast series of organic chemical compounds, the exact identities of which we need not worry about here. Some of these exist in the grape, others are formed during fermentation, while others are the result of maturation. Those that begin in the grape are mostly to be found in the skins, or just under the skins. Skin contact is increasingly being used by white wine producers to extract more flavour. However, if you taste the must before it is turned into wine, it will not taste of the characters that we expect from the particular grape.

Dr Ann C. Noble, working at the University of California, Davis (campus), has developed an aroma wheel to assist tasters in their descriptions. This only categorises the smells and the flavours of wine, and no attempt is made to assess structure, but it is very helpful. The wheel has three levels, starting in the middle with

when tasting it is important to let the different parts of the mouth do their bit, so take a reasonable mouthful of wine

Tastes

Bitter

Sour (acidity)

Salt

Sweet

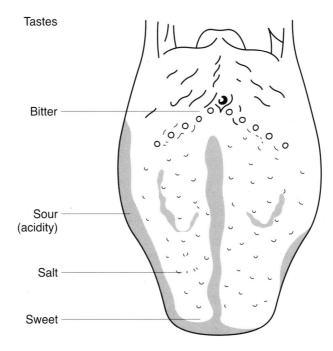

different parts of the tongue detect different tastes

broad categories and the aromas get more specific as you work outwards. For example, a wine might be described as fruity, and then the type of fruit, say citrus, and then the specific fruit, e.g. lemon or grapefruit.

The palate

The palate is, oddly, not very useful in itself for tasting. We get the retro-olfactory effects as the wine warms up in the mouth, but the tongue, gums and soft palate are capable of detecting only four basic tastes – sweet, sour, bitter and salt. The mouth is, however, the place where we assess the wine's structure – the balance of sweetness, acid, alcohol and tannin that goes to make wine more than just a flavour.

The good news is that because the mouth detects different tastes in different places, a small sip is not enough; you will need to take a reasonable mouthful. Once you have the wine in your mouth, you should allow the palate to do its work. This is where professional wine tasting becomes an entertaining spectator sport for the uninitiated, with highly amusing facial expressions, strange slurping noises that your mother told you not to make in polite company, and ultimately, expectoration of sometimes the finest of wine, without drinking a drop.

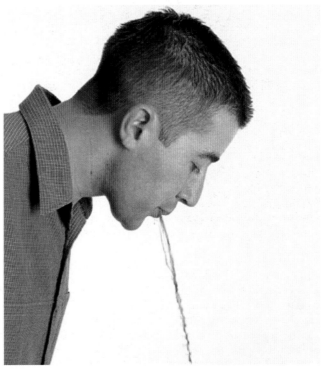

when a number of wines are to be assessed, spitting becomes essential

Sweetness and acidity

Sweetness is the first taste you will notice, because the taste buds that detect this are mostly concentrated at the front or on the tip of the tongue. Of all the tastes in wine this is the easiest to identify, if only because we are far more practised in looking for sweetness from an early age. Sweets and ripe fruit are part of our childhood experiences. We will see how sweet and sweetish wines are made later in this book. Our assessment of sweetness is not totally straightforward, however. Sometimes a wine that has very ripe fruit will seem sweeter than it really is, while a sweeter wine with high acidity can seem drier than chemical analysis would show.

Acidity

Acidity is next. Wine is one of the most acidic of alcoholic drinks, significantly higher in acidity than beer or spirits, but this high level of acid is vital for balance. We detect acidity at the sides of our tongue; it comes across as a mouth-watering sensation.

Because of the importance of acidity, we will look at it in more detail at the end of this section.

Tannin

Tannin can give a bitter taste to a wine, but like alcohol and body, its main effect is felt rather than tasted. Tannin is a vital part of the structure and mouthfeel of all red wines, and occasionally crops up in whites, especially those that have seen new oak casks. It exhibits itself as a mouth-drying sensation, sticking your lips to your gums, and drying the tongue and top of the mouth. We will look at this further later in the chapter.

Bitterness and salt

The only other tastes that we can detect on the palate are bitterness and saltiness. Few wines are in any way salty, the major example being Sherry which can have a salty tang, especially if matured in Sanlucar de Barrameda. We will return to this in the chapter on fortified wine tasting.

Bitterness can occur in wines. It is generally seen as a negative comment in tasting, although it can be part of the effect of tannin and seen as a positive attribute.

The other palate characteristics are more to do with the sense of feeling than of taste. These are body and alcohol.

Body

The body, or mouthfeel, of a wine is an assessment of how light or heavy the wine feels in the mouth. Mouthfeel is not directly related to the alcohol level, but generally higher alcohol wines, such as Californian Zinfandels will feel heavier on the mouth than cooler climate white wines where the alcohol level is lower.

Alcohol

Ethanol, or ethyl alcohol, is the main alcohol in wine. It is detected by a warming sensation on the sides of the tongue. All wine must have some alcohol, the level is usually between eight and 15 per cent of the volume, but can be higher or lower. Whatever the level, it should be in balance with the other components, and should not stand out as being excessively high or low. Very high alcohol levels, around 14 per cent and above, can contribute a sweet flavour to wine, which is why some very ripe wines can appear sweeter even though analysis proves they are dry.

Spit or swallow

When you taste a few wines over dinner you will be expecting to drink them and enjoy the pleasurable effect of a, hopefully moderate, consumption of ethanol. That is, after all, what wine is all about. It is a beverage.

At a formal tasting, however, you may well be presented with dozens of wines, sometimes hundreds of samples. Even the merest sip of each would result in severe inebriation, or worse. Professionals and keen amateurs must, therefore, get over their intrinsic distaste of spitting.

Some wine merchants have developed their skill almost into an art form, with high-velocity trajectories that will hit the middle of any given spittoon from the other side of the room. Such virtuoso performances are impressive, but not essential. All you need to be able to do is eject the

wine from your mouth in a clean manner without spraying or dribbling. Practise in the bath.

Be aware that however practised you are, you will almost certainly swallow some. There are no recognized averages for the amount swallowed because it will vary from individual to individual, but bear this in mind if you are attending a large tasting, particularly if fortified wines are being shown, and you intend to drive home afterwards.

Acidity

Although the mention of acidity can be off-putting for the beginner, with connotations of sourness and harshness, it is a vital part of the structure of wine, holding the flavour together and balancing the other components, making it a refreshing drink and acting as a preservative. Wine is one of the most acidic of alcoholic beverages. Occasionally the acidity is too high and the wine is unbalanced, tart and harsh, but equally, if too low, the wine will taste flat and the flavours will be lost.

Acid in wine can come from three possible sources. The first, and by far the most important, are the natural fruit acids of the grape, and we will consider these in the greatest detail. If the fruit is low in natural acid the wine maker can augment it with additional acid; ideally, this should not be noticeable in the finished product. The third source is spoilage, which produces a different type of acid. We will look at this in Chapter 13.

Natural fruit acids

Underripe grapes are hard and have a very high level of acid. As the grape reaches veraison and begins to ripen, the flesh becomes softer, the skin changes colour from blueish-green to either a more yellow hue or purple-black, and the sugar level increases. At the same time the concentration of acidity falls. This happens partly because of dilution by other components, and partly by chemical changes that result from photosynthesis.

Two different acids dominate: malic and tartaric. In underripe grapes, malic is the major acid, with tartaric becoming more important as the grape ripens. During their training wine makers go to extraordinary lengths to learn the difference in tastes of these acids, but for our purpose the important fact is that malic acid is far stronger an acid that tartaric. Strictly in chemical terms, each malic acid molecule has two acid groups, compared to one on each tartaric acid molecule.

In very warm climates, the grape gains sugars very rapidly but often this is accompanied by an excessive drop in acidity. Additions of tartaric acid are quite normal in such places as Australia and California, and in the hot, southern European vineyard areas.

Acid reduction

Wine makers can also reduce acidity in wines where it is felt to be excessive. This can be done by simply neutralizing the acidity using a suitable alkali, or by using biological means. The first will have no effect on the flavour of the finished product, apart from reducing the mouth-watering character; the latter, called malo-lactic fermentation, adds extra flavour complexity too.

Malo-lactic fermentation is the traditional way of reducing acidity. Lactic acid bacteria, either naturally occurring in the winery or inoculated into the wine, convert the harsh, green-apple malic acid into the softer-tasting lactic acid, the acid found in milk products. The effect is to reduce the total acidity. At the same time a series of by-products is produced, the most important of which is the chemical diacetyl. This has a buttery or creamy flavour and is responsible for the buttery character so often attributed to Chardonnay.

Balance

Acidity is vital to the balance of flavour and structure in any wine. A balanced wine is one in which none of the component parts dominates. Sweetness and acidity balance each other on the palate so they need to be looked at together when assessing sweeter styles of wine.

Sweet wines need a higher degree of acidity if they are to be well balanced. A medium or sweet wine with low acid will be sickly and cloying, whereas one with a high level of acidity will finish clean without that overly sweet character.

This balancing effect is used by wine makers to give balance to wines that might otherwise be too tart. Many German wines, and those from other cool climate areas, benefit from a small addition of unfermented grape juice after fermentation to balance the naturally high acidity.

The crisp wines of Vinho Verde in Portugal are sold bone dry in their native country but are often sweetened slightly for the export markets, particularly when sold to cooler, northern countries where the natural freshness of the palate, so enjoyable in the region, can seem too harsh. Many inexpensive wines from other countries aimed at beginner wine drinkers are similarly sweetened. This blending, which has to be done with care, goes by various names – Süssreserve in Germany, back-blending in the New World.

Tasting acidity

The most convenient acid to use for this exercise is lemon juice. It is not ideal because lemon juice is very high in citric acid, not an acid found naturally in grapes, and of course it has a very distinctive flavour. However, we are looking at the effects here, not the tastes, so try to ignore the flavour. Tartaric acid can be used if you can get hold of it.

Mix up a dilute citric acid solution using lemon juice and neutral bottled water. A couple of teaspoonfuls in a tasting measure of water will be fine, there is no need to be too precise. Take a small amount in a tasting glass and taste it, swilling it all around the mouth as usual. Think about what is happening in the mouth, and notice where you are feeling the effect, almost certainly down the sides of the tongue. Think about what is happening in your mouth, feel the saliva building up – acid is mouth-watering.

when thinking about acidity, think about lemon juice

Next, consider the effect acid and sweetness have on one another. Dissolve a teaspoonful of sugar in a mug of water. Granulated sugar is fine, although technically the sugar in sweet wine is the sweeter-tasting fructose. Take two tasting glasses. Put some of the sweet solution in one, and some of the sweet solution mixed half-and-half with the lemon juice mixture in the other. Compare their tastes. Notice how the acidity covers up some of the sweetness – the same happens in wine.

Tannin

Along with colour, tannin is extracted from the skins of black grapes during the fermentation process, which is why it is rarely found in white wines, where the skins are generally discarded before fermentation. It can also come from stalks and pips during fermentation. As well as adding to the palate and general feel of the wine, tannin is one of the essential preservatives in wine. If a red wine is going to be cellared for a long time it must start off with a high level of tannin. This makes some reds very harsh and austere in their youth, but it enables them to survive and develop over time. Wines such as cru classé claret and Barolo are hugely tannic when young. Contrariwise, there are many wines made for early consumption where a high level of tannin would be inappropriate. The classic example is Beaujolais Nouveau, but today many others also exist. The big-selling American and Australian branded wines such as Gallo and Jacob's Creek are not meant to be aged, and so are made with relatively low tannin levels.

Fortunately for the wine maker and marketeer, colour and tannin are not extracted at the same time. Usually the colouring components of the grape are extracted first, with the tannin following. A wine maker can, therefore, make deep-coloured, low-tannin reds by removing the skins earlier. A wine for immediate consumption may have the skins macerated in the new wine for a week or so, whereas the longer-life wine may spend as long as a month in contact with the cap of skins.

White wines generally do not spend a long time in contact with the skins. Tannin in white wine comes when new oak casks are used for fermentation and maturation. These tannins are extracted from the oak.

The tannic harshness that you will find in young Barolo or immature claret when tasted without food will disappear if you take the wine alongside protein. The wine trade's maxim, 'a food wine', often derided by wine journalists as meaning out of balance, is really meant to indicate a wine that will be best enjoyed when part of the meal. Wine-producing countries and regions with strong culinary traditions that include wine with food, such as France, Italy and Spain, tend to make wines like this. Wine makers in Germany, and those making the big Australian brands, intend their wines to be enjoyed as drinks in their own right, so they may not work as well with food.

To get the full feel of tannin brew a strong cup of tea. Place a teabag in a cup of boiling water and leave it there until the water is cool, then taste it. The mouth-puckering dryness is the result of the tannin. (Research has shown that both tea and red wine contain large quantities of antioxidants so this tannic effect is good for you.)

To experience the effect of different tannin levels in different wines, taste a Beaujolais, thinking about the mouth-drying sensation. For the greatest contrast, choose a Beaujolais Nouveau but be aware this will put a limit on when you can do the tasting. Standard Beaujolais, or one labelled Beaujolais Villages, will do just as well, and the latter will be a more satisfying drink. At first you may find that the tannin level seems fairly high, but then go on to taste a Barolo. (For the moment, we will ignore the rest of the tasting note.) The difference is enormous. The Barolo will be mouth-puckeringly tannic.

Note also that both the wines are quite high in acidity, particularly the Barolo. This combination of acidity and tannin when taken to excess leads to astringency in the wine. If you found the Barolo too astringent, try it again with a slice of salami, or some Gorgonzola cheese. Notice how the structure gives way, how both the tannin and acidity disappear when fat and protein are present, allowing the flavours to shine through. Many wines from traditional European wine areas are meant to go with food, and as a result do not always show well when tasted on their own.

writing tasting notes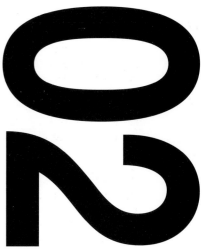

Our memories are horribly fallible, in wine tasting as in everything else in life. Can you remember, with precision, what you had for dinner a week last Tuesday, or what you were doing on June 3 last year? However good a memory you have, writing notes about wine is essential. There are occasional exceptions; some trade professionals are able to recall exactly what a particular wine tasted like years after the event, but such experts are rare. Moreover, they will usually be selective either in their tasting – perhaps specialists in a particular field where they taste the same type of wine, or even the same wine, regularly and often enough for it to be engraved on their memory – or selective in their memory – remembering the highlights but not the dozens of other wines in between. For the rest of us there are notebooks.

The purpose of a note depends on the purpose of the tasting. One, now retired, blender is reputed to have habitually written 'good wine' for the first wine on the bench and simply 'as above' for all the others in a flight (the range of wines in a tasting) – but he was selecting for blend, and the wines should have been pre-selected to match a specification. Judges in competitions reduce their notes to scores. No one will ever read the comments, usually only the winners will ever be revealed even to the judges, so why bother with unnecessary work? An example of a judge's score sheet from the International Wine & Spirits competition is shown on the next page.

At the other end of the scale are the retailers and journalists whose prose is designed to encourage purchasers, or entertain readers. Here purple prose is required to keep the reader entertained; comments such as delicate as a butterfly, or full-bodied as a sumo wrestler, have their place.

Then there are the serious students of wine who have to impress their examiners, not with florid language and unmitigated praise but with their knowledge and experience. They have to show that they have looked at the various components, and that through good judgement they are able to draw valid conclusions about the wines' origins, maturity or value.

Your personal notes should act primarily as an *aide-mémoire* for the wines you have tasted, and your impressions of them. As you develop your wine knowledge it is important that you write as much as possible about the wine – the more you taste the more you will be able to write. These notes will eventually build up into a valuable resource but its value is in its use. Do remember to refer back to your notes occasionally, otherwise they are just a waste of effort and paper. You will find it helpful if you write your notes systematically in an organized manner.

Systematic tasting notes

To this end, the Wine and Spirit Education Trust (WSET), the largest product-knowledge-based wine education body in the world, has developed the Systematic Approach to Tasting. This was developed in consultation with senior members of the UK wine trade to encourage

MARKING SHEET

Judge: ....   Flight Number: ....

Date: ....   Category: ....

Country: ....

Sample Number (Sparkling)	Appearance (10) (20)	Nose (30) (25)	Palate (35) (30)	Overall Balance (25) (25)	Total (100)	Comments

Gold = 85+   Silver = 75+   Bronze = 65+   Under 50 = Defective please state reasons   Commended = over 70 if not G/S/B

students of the subject to write full notes. WSET students at Advanced Certificate and Diploma use these as part of the learning process, as do examination candidates worldwide. Because there are currently three levels of the course, the system consists of three progressive lists, one for each syllabus level developing from the beginners' through to Diploma level. All three checklists are reproduced at the end of the book.

As you will see, each list covers the main components of taste, in the order in which most people will detect them, with extra levels of detail added at each stage so that with regular use a library with full descriptions of each wine tasted can be built up. At each level, the chart consists of two columns; the first listing the observations, the second giving examples of the vocabulary you might want to use. The examples are just that, examples – do not try to restrict your notes to the words used here. If a wine is fruity, then try to identify the type of fruit, if spicy then what spice. Use as many terms as are appropriate; some wines are simple and one-dimensional, better than ordinary wines have a whole basketful of different

flavours, leading to complexity and interest. There is immense value in covering all aspects of the wines tasted, especially when learning about wine. Candidates taking the WSET examinations are required to know the first column and use it in the test, but even the keen amateur will find the structure useful because it promotes discipline in tasting. The structure of the wine, the backbone of acidity, tannin and alcohol are at least as important to the enjoyment of wine as the flavours that the wine journalists talk about so much, especially when blind tasting or thinking about matching food and wine.

Use of the systematic approach

Using the Intermediate Certificate chart as a guide is recommended. This covers the main flavour and structure components of every wine descriptively, without calling for any complex assessment. You will find details of the various headings in Chapter 1. The only part that perhaps needs any explanation is the conclusion – at this level a basic assessment of quality. The scale used is somewhat limiting, covering as it does only three grades. The three points on the published scale need to be looked at in detail:

- 'Poor' means faulty, something is wrong with the wine, or it completely fails to live up to expectations. The last decision is one you will be able to take with experience of each wine style. Initially try to look at all wines against a background of the world range of wines made; a wine that the expert considers disappointing for its type can still be fundamentally good.

- 'Acceptable' means the wine is OK, but that is probably the most complimentary comment you can make about it. Most big-selling branded wines and, these days, most cheap wines, will come into this category. An acceptable wine is one you would not mind drinking, but you would choose an alternative if you could.

- 'Good' is a catchall category for everything else.

If there is a criticism of the system, it is that this is far too broad a spectrum. This is addressed in the Advanced Certificate checklist, where commercial value comes into your assessment. Of course you are completely free to include whatever additional comments you want; anything from 'Yes, let's buy lots of it', to 'Avoid like the plague'. For your own purposes you will probably want to think of value for money as well as quality, and the food the wine will complement.

The Advanced Certificate adds a few extra headings to consider. Under 'Appearance' you are asked for a description of rim versus core in order that you can write a fuller description of the way the wine looks. This is far more important with red wines than white, which tend to fade to a water-white rim anyway, but the rim and core difference is important for many old white wines, and for many sweet and fortified wines. The core indicates the depth of colour and the rim gives you an impression of the true colour of the wine, and in doing so gives an impression of its maturity. Remember this is *not* the same as age.

The nose adds 'development'. Deciding whether a wine smells youthful or aged is something that comes with more practice and is therefore omitted from the Intermediate Certificate list. The addition on the palate is alcohol. Correctly judging the level of alcohol is not always easy and there is no need to attempt to give the exact degree of alcohol. Most wines fall into the 'medium' category here, light and high are really the exceptions. Note the use of the word light rather than low here – this is because the term 'low alcohol' has a very specific legal definition in many countries.

The biggest difference at Advanced Certificate is, not surprisingly, in the Conclusions. With greater experience you will want to say more about the wine than simply poor or good. At the very least you will want to qualify your assessment of quality – good for its type or not. You are asked to assess the market segment into which the wine falls. If you bought the wine and are not tasting it blind, you will already know this, but it is the most important decision to make if you are tasting blind. Even if you know what the sample is, you will want to think about its quality in relation to its peers, so link the overall quality assessment to the market category. An inexpensive wine can still be a stunning example for its price, and a Grand Cru Chablis might be a poor, good or stunning example of Grand Cru Chablis. State of maturity is an assessment of the wine's drinkability and ability to age. Is it ready now? Should it have been drunk by now, or does it need more time? If the latter, then how long? Just another year or two, or should I lay this down for my grandchildren?

The Diploma level requires much more detailed conclusions, as befits the level of the qualification. The quality assessment has to be made with reference to the type of wine under consideration, and in the examination this should be justified by reference to the tasting note and the characters of the wine. In the examination, of course, the wines are shown 'Unspecified', that is blind – with no information supplied about them – or 'Partially Specified', with some information given, usually the region and sometimes the grape variety. For example, a candidate may come to the conclusion that a particular wine comes from the southern Rhône and the assessment of quality might read something like this:

Good quality for a Côtes-du-Rhône Villages wine because of the peppery character and high level of alcohol backed up with intense fruit flavours and firm but ripe tannin structure. Too structured and intense to be a mere basic Côtes-du-Rhône, yet without the power and complexity to be a single cru level wine.

The assessment of maturity too needs more detail. Candidates are required to say not only ready to drink, or needs time, but to put a timescale on that. So this wine might be described as ready now but will continue to improve for a further year and hold for one or two years after that, again, backed up by referring to the wine where appropriate.

In a sommeliers' examination the conclusion would probably also include a very specific food recommendation because this is the most important part of the sommeliers' role. For most of us, too, this is an important aspect of why we taste.

Reading notes

For most people wine tasting is a hobby, not an examination. Reading your notes after you have made them will certainly help you learn what styles of wine are made in various places, or what a particular grape variety tastes like. From a practical point of view the most important reason for taking notes is to remember whether or not you want to buy a second bottle.

Taking this to its logical conclusion, the two most important parts of any tasting note are the details of the wine and your personal comments. What was it and did I like it are the only things most wine tasters need to remember for the majority of the wines they taste.

When not to write full notes

As your tasting skill and note writing develop, you will find that you do not need to use the full list for every wine. If, for example, you are tasting a flight of young Chablis or New Zealand Sauvignon Blancs, the pale colour and crisp acidity will be more or less consistent from one to another, and should be taken as read. You need only comment when something is out of the ordinary. You can, however, make finer distinctions between samples. In such cases, your notes can concentrate on the differences between the wines rather than their standard structure.

Wine by numbers

Scoring wine is a subject in its own right, with numerous different scoring systems in use. Wine scores, particularly those of certain commentators and major wine

magazines, have become part of wine mythology. On the surface they appear to make life so much simpler for the consumer – an easy way of comparing the quality of two or more wines without having to spend vast amounts of money buying a bottle of each.

Some tasters score every wine they see, others only if judging competitions. Some use a scale of one to 100, others one to ten, and many one to 20. In many cases the first half of the scale is irrelevant as anything scoring, for example, less than 50 on the Parker scale is undrinkable (Robert Parker Jr is an influential American wine judge and critic who publishes *The Wine Advocate*. His marking scale is nominally 0–100, but anything scoring under 50 is faulty). Some people score wines on an absolute scale, so that a cheap wine, however good it is in its market segment, will never get a high score. Others score within type, so wines of a particular type and price are judged together. If you want to score wines you will need to develop your own system, and stick with it.

In simple terms a 'Parker' or a 'Wine Spectator' score of 100 is as close to perfect as any wine will ever be (and, incidentally, will become almost unobtainable and will cost an arm and leg – whatever it is – as soon as the scores are published.) A wine getting 50 is flawed in some way, so in fact the scale is only out of 50. Clearly, within the parameters set, an 89 is better than an 85, and we can all understand why – but should wine be reduced to numbers?

There are, however, a number of difficulties with wine scores. In most cases the score is based on one, probably the most recent, tasting. (Robert Parker uses an average taken over a range of tastings.) They show, therefore, a snapshot of the wine. But wines develop and change, not always predictably, and a taster's impression can be altered by where in the line-up a particular wine has been placed.

Use numbers if you prefer, but treat them with care. The one place that a wine's score is very important is in wine investment – but that is a subject too big to be included here.

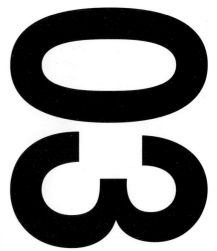

aromatic white wines

Most of us start our wine drinking careers with white wines. Whether a medium-dry fruity Liebfraumilch from Germany, a fizzy Lambrusco or rich, up-front Australian Chardonnay, white wines seem to offer security and safety to the novice drinker. They are not threatening in the way that a harsh, tannic red might be, and there seems to be less rigmarole and mystique attached. White wine seems, on the surface, to be simpler and more straightforward.

White wines offer the consumer a vast range of different flavours and styles. Some, such as Frascati and Muscadet, make a virtue of their neutrality, while the heady spice-island perfume of a Gewürztraminer, or the pungent oak of a modern Chardonnay, make the wines unmissably assertive. In sweetness too, whites offer a far greater range than reds. Red wine is mostly dry, only a handful are anything but, but white wine can be bone dry, through medium to fully sweet. Since aromatic dry wines are the easiest to recognize, we will start with these.

Aromatic dry whites

The aromatic qualities of the wines considered here come from the grape. No clever wine making, no complex character from wood ageing, just preservation of the natural attributes of the flavours in those delicate compounds that make certain white grapes special. Grapes such as Sauvignon Blanc, Riesling – and many of its offspring, Gewürztraminer and Muscat – cannot help but make themselves noticed in the wine. With grapes like this it is the variety that gives the lead. The region, the climate and soil, the 'terroir' are important, but of less significance to the final style than the raw material. Because of this, we will consider the wine by variety, and since few are ever blended, we can still cover all bases.

Sauvignon Blanc

Of all the aromatic varieties, it is Sauvignon that has taken the world by storm. While Riesling and Muscat remain resolutely unfashionable, Sauvignon Blanc has become trendy and chic, the wine to be seen with – especially if it comes from New Zealand.

Unblended Sauvignon, usually produces pale-coloured dry wines with marked, refreshing acidity and a powerful, sometimes pungent nose of grass, elderflower and gooseberries, sometimes described as 'cats' pee', an aroma all too familiar to anyone who has ever lived with a tom cat. These aromas are, despite the descriptors used, attractive, appealing and very inviting. They are young smells – Sauvignon is not a variety to keep locked away in a dusty cellar. Drink the wines when they are a year or two old, while they still have vibrancy and youthful exuberance. Some of these wines will simply fall apart with age, others will hold together but lose freshness, and it is that very liveliness that makes them so delicious.

Like most 'noble' grapes, Sauvignon comes originally from France, from two regions specifically, the Loire and Bordeaux. In the latter it is used to add refreshing acidity to the sweet wines of Sauternes and Barsac, as well as the neighbouring regions of Loupiac, St Croix du Mont and, just outside the Bordeaux area, Montbazillac. In the Loire, Sauvignon goes to make the fine, racy wines of what is known as the central vineyards – Sancerre and Pouilly Fumé and their less famous neighbours, Quincy, Reuilly and Mennetou-Salon.

Not many years ago anyone writing this book would have directed readers straight to Sancerre and Pouilly-Fumé for benchmark Sauvignon. Now the advice would be to go for a New Zealand Sauvignon, in particular, one from Marlborough. Here, at the northern end of New Zealand's South Island, this grape comes into its own, producing wines more pungent and with greater varietal character than anywhere else. Similar, if lighter, styles are now available from all over the world, South African and Chilean being the closest in style.

For a different view of Sauvignon, try one from California. Whereas the rest of the world tends to try to preserve the primary fruit flavours of Sauvignon, some US wine makers use oak both in fermentation and maturation of Sauvignon. This bigger, richer style can be quite a shock after the fruit-driven styles from other parts.

Gewürztraminer

In a blind tasting it is Gewürztraminer above all others that tasters hope for. Of all grape varieties there is none as perfumed, as seductive and easy to recognize as this. The Germanic-sounding name – spelt without the umlaut

in France – belies its Italian origins. In the Etsch Valley in the Italian Tyrol there is a town called Termeno, or Tramin in the local Germanic dialect. (This area was once part of Austria.) Traminer means simply the grapes of Tramin, and Gewürztraminer is the most perfumed version of it, *Gewürz* being German for spice.

To be fair to the grape, spice is one flavour that rarely appears in Gewürztraminer tasting notes. The wines can be pungent and aromatic, with a rose-water or tropical fruit character, most notably lychee or rambutan.

Gewürztraminer is a red grape, not black as would produce a red wine, but the skins have a distinc red hue to them, as does its neighbour in Alsace, the Pinot Gris. This coloured skin results in deep-coloured wines, often pale gold rather than the lemon yellow of most white wine.

Viognier

Twenty years ago Viognier accounted for about 32 hectares of the world's vineyards, nearly all in three small communes in France. Even that was an increase on the area 20 years before. Now the plantings of Viognier are growing faster than any other variety. It is generally seen as a difficult grape to grow and ripen, which accounts for its previous unpopularity, but the quality of its fruit has finally come to the attention of wine lovers all over.

Underripe Viognier produces a pleasant but bland white wine, but given long enough on the vine the flavours develop. Initially floral, further ripening will give characters of white peach and overripe apricot and, if left still longer, a distinct ginger spice develops.

Viognier's natural home is the northern Rhône where it is the only variety for the neighbouring appellations of Condrieu and Château Grillet. It also plays an important role in the red wines of Côte Rôtie, giving the wine a scent of violets and lifting the bold Syrah fruit. From there it has been exported to the south of France, Australia and California, among other places.

In the south of France it cannot be used for appellation contrôlée wines but is often seen as a Vin de Pays, often very aromatic because of the heat of the Mediterranean sun. In Australia the Viognier story is intimately tied in with Yalumba, who first considered growing Viognier in the early 1970s when it was decided to try it in the Barossa Valley alongside their Shiraz. The first plantings were in 1979 but it was not until the mid-to-late 1990s that the wine makers really understood how to make great wine from them. Further growth of the variety in Australia has been very much the result of investment by Yalumba as they have a commercial nursery that has supplied almost all the antipodean cuttings. Most Californian Viognier too was planted in the last few years of the twentieth century. Unusually for the variety, current American examples are often heavily oaked.

Muscat

Tasting notes are littered with all manner of fruits – blackcurrants, gooseberries, raspberries, lychees, tropical fruit . . . the list goes on. One fruit almost conspicuous by its absence is the grape. Wine is made from grapes, but rarely smells or tastes of grapes. The one exception is Muscat. There are many different spellings, many subtly different clones or sub-varieties of Muscat, but they all taste of grapes. Many of the most famous Muscats are sweet, often through early fortification, and some are bubbly, but there are still-dry versions too. Alsace in eastern France produces the most famous, but equally dry wines are available elsewhere – Australia and Portugal being particularly notable.

Pinot Gris

It is debatable whether Pinot Gris should appear here or under neutral wines in Chapter 4, for the refreshing, thirst-quenching bottle of Pinot Grigio served up with pasta at the local trattoria is miles away from the heady, oily richness of a Grand Cru 'Tokay' Pinot Gris from Alsace. It is the latter style that earns Pinot Gris its place among the aromatics.

Like Gewürztraminer, Pinot Gris is a red-skinned grape (it is a natural mutation of the Burgundian Pinot Noir), used for white wines. The most aromatic styles are those from the picturesque hillside vineyards of Alsace where the protective Vosges mountains ensure plenty of sunshine to ripen the grapes. When yields are kept down, as they are in particular for the prestige examples, the wines can take on a character not unlike Gewürztraminer – perfumed and spicy – but with slightly higher acidity. Normally dry to off-dry, there are also sweet Pinot Gris made in this region.

Across the Rhine in Germany the wine is called either Rülander or Grauburgunder. One indicates a dry style of the wine, the other a medium-dry, but confusingly there appears to be no consistency at all among producers as to which way round they should be. One producer's Rülander might be dry, another's medium.

Few New World countries have planted much Pinot Gris. There have been some very successful plantings in New Zealand, and in the Pacific Northwest of the United States – Oregon and Washington State. At their best these have full, rich texture and aromatic qualities. Pinot Grigio – the Italian for Pinot Gris – is so unlike the others we will revisit it in another section.

Riesling

Riesling suffers an odd fate. The *cognosenti* are universally agreed that Riesling is the world's greatest grape variety, yet it remains resolutely unfashionable with the wine-consuming public. Its greatness is only manifest when grown in the right place, as Riesling, like the Princess in the story of the Princess and the Pea, is picky as to site. All of Germany's most spectacular vineyard sites are given over to Riesling, it is considered the best grape in Alsace, and it is the dry Rieslings from Wachau that Austrian connoisseurs prize above the rest of the country's wine. If imitation is the most sincere form of flattery then Riesling is the most flattered grape for all over the world grape growers have taken its name in vain. From the Laski or Olasz Rizlings of Eastern Europe, to South Africa's Cape Riesling (the rather bland Crouchen Blanc), the American Emerald Riesling and Australian Hunter Riesling, other grapes bask in the glory of the name, but in doing so devalue it beyond measure.

What makes Riesling so special is its amazing aromatic character, its ability to ripen, occasionally to vast sugar levels, without losing acidity, and its ability to age and develop unmatched by any other variety. Long, mild autumns allow a slow accumulation of flavours that do not need any clever tricks from the wine maker. There is no need to overlay the fruit with oak, no need to add buttery characters with malo-lactic fermentation. Riesling's fine fruit, balanced with its backbone of clean, natural fruit acidity, needs no make-up to look good.

Perhaps the world's greatest Rieslings are not dry but the medium and sweet wines of Germany and Alsace, but Germany does produce some outstanding dry Rieslings, and many Alsace wines are dry. In Germany look out for 'trocken' on the label or wine list – but do not get confused with Trockenbeerenauslese which is at the other end of the sweetness scale altogether. Many Rieslings from the southern regions of Germany such as Pfalz and Baden are full-flavoured enough not to need the sweetness that we have become accustomed to from Germany. Further north the Charter Group in the Rheingau make a point of producing dry Riesling wines, many of which are so austere in their youth that they would put off all but the most ardent fan, but with a few years' bottle age they develop and show great concentration of pure Riesling fruit. In Alsace, most wines labelled Riesling will be dry, or at least close to it. Sweeter styles are made, but generally they are labelled as such – see Chapter 7.

Despite the misuse of the name, there are some very good true Rieslings available from New World countries. In Australia the premium areas are Clare and Eden Valleys, both hot by comparison to the Mosel and thus giving higher alcohol content and different styles. Classic tasting notes for Clare Riesling usually include 'lime-like' and the wines can certainly have the refreshing quality of Rose's Lime Juice, both in flavour and structure, for the vine manages to retain its vibrant acidity, even in this heat. New Zealand makes some excellent late-harvest Rieslings which, being sweet, the legislators in Brussels won't let us in the EU taste, and dry wines which have a distinct pungency about them that makes them taste almost like Sauvignon.

Chenin Blanc

Like Pinot Gris, Chenin deserves its place here because of one or two wines, in this case Savennières and the occasional Vouvray Sec. The grape is something of a schizophrenic variety since beyond these it can make some stunning sweet and medium-sweet wines if the weather permits, and does produce tanker-loads of bland dry white wine perfect for the barbecue but lost in a wine tasting.

It is difficult to pin down the exact character of Chenin yet it is very distinct – slightly musty, maybe honeyed and certainly floral (but what flower?). Some tasters find smells of wet wool or wet dog, others describe it as lanolin. Chenin, whether dry or sweet, will always have a streak of fresh acidity like Riesling and for this reason, along perhaps with the floral character, they are often confused.

Scheurebe

This unusual grape deserves far greater attention but at the moment its lack of fame makes it one of the best value aromatic dry whites – top, single estate Scheurebes are in the same league as the best Sancerres or Marlborough Sauvignons, at two-thirds of the price. Pronounced 'sh-oi-ray-ber' it was developed by Georg Scheu in 1916. The basic style is similar to Sauvignon, being pungently aromatic with very intense fruit on the palate, held together by a backbone of acidity and alcohol, but the flavours here are more akin to blackcurrant and grapefruit than gooseberries and asparagus. The best are German, and in particular from the Pfalz, but they are a million miles away from the semi-sweet, light floral style that is most people's idea of German wine.

Get to know your grapes – identification of wine styles

The wine list:

As an initial exercise try to identify the fundamental style of each of the varieties listed. Set up a tasting of the following wines:

- An inexpensive New Zealand (Marlborough Region) Sauvignon Blanc. For this exercise it need not be expensive, or a single estate. One of the big-selling brands like Cooks or Montana will be fine. Choose the youngest you can find, preferably this year's, or at the oldest last year's wine.

- Scheurebe is grown in other countries but Germany is the most important. Select a good, single estate version made from well-ripened grapes. Look for Kabinett or Spätlese on the label, but for this tasting also look for 'trocken' – dry. If you can find it, Lingenfelder's is one of the best, and is not too expensive.

- For the Riesling go either to Alsace or to the southern-most parts of Germany, Pfalz or Baden. Look out for a trocken wine, but note that these are often disguised – a brand such as Devil's Rock will be fine, but it looks like an Australian variety with its modern label.

- Alsace Gewürztraminer, again, need not be a very expensive version, but avoid the very cheapest. Pay about the same as for the Sauvignon, and again, buy young.

- Aromatic Pinot Gris really only comes from Alsace. Try to find an example from Trimbach to demonstrate the grapes at their driest and yet with great intensity; many of the other producers make an off-dry version. Avoid anything labelled Sélèction de Grains Nobles (SGN) or Vandange Tardive – they will be good but fit into another tasting.

- Viognier can be very expensive but a Vin de Pays d'Oc version, or the slightly pricier Oxford Landing Viognier from Yalumba will show the grape's character, perhaps even better than the most expensive Condrieu.

- A good quality Vouvray will not be cheap, so again pay a little more to be guaranteed the varietal characteristic. All too many Chenin Blanc wines are bland, so it is worth the extra.

- Steering clear of the innumerable sweet and sparkling Muscats available leaves a limited choice. Again Alsace comes to the rescue, but these are rare and therefore expensive. The Australians, and in particular Brown Brothers in Victoria, have carved out a particular niche for themselves with dry Muscats, or you might be able to track down one of the Palmela Muscats from J. P. Vinhos in Setúbal, Portugal. Peter Bright, an Australian-trained wine maker working in the UK, has developed these from the local Muscat that would otherwise have gone to make the local sweet fortified wine.

Tasting guidance

As discussed in Chapter 1, the first observation is the appearance. Note the pale, almost water-white appearance of the Sauvignon, Riesling and Muscat compared to the much deeper, perhaps almost golden hue of the Scheurebe, Viognier and especially the Gewürztraminer. Pinot Gris will probably be on the deeper side, but this varies according to the producer, and the Chenin will probably be between the two.

Next, following the guidance in Chapter 1, taste the wines. Make notes of the nose and palate of each, taking care to find the differences. Do not worry about vocabulary – note what you think each smells and tastes of. There are standard terms in common use in the wine trade for each of these, but use terms that mean something to you.

Typically you will find the following:

- Pungent gooseberries, 'cat's pee', grass or elderflower for Sauvignon, with marked acidity on the palate.

- Scheurebe too is very pungent, but has a more citric, particularly grapefruit flavour.

- Floral or mineral for Riesling when young, again with high acidity.

- Very open, perfumed nose with hints of tropical fruit – lychees in particular on the Gewürztraminer. Note also the elevated alcohol and lower acidity than before.

- Pinot Gris can easily be confused with Gewürztraminer. Again perfumed but less so, and with a more oily character, and higher acidity.

- Viognier's flavours depend on when the grape was picked, but look out for floral or peach flavours, perhaps giving way to ginger and all-spice on riper versions. Like Gewürztraminer, it is almost always high in alcohol, and the acidity is typically neither particularly high nor low.

- Chenin Blanc is often described as wet wool, but can be honeyed, even when the wine is dry. Lanolin is another popular descriptor.

- Muscat is one of very few wines that smells and tastes of grapes. Young Muscat has a nose reminiscent of white peaches, perfumed soap or bathsalts. Note that it smells as if it is going to be sweet, and yet, the wines listed above are dry.

Advanced level

Sauvignon masterclass

Compare the almost overpowering character of a premium, unoaked Sauvignon from a top producer (expect to pay twice as much as the big brand mentioned above) with the much more restrained style from Sancerre or Pouilly Fumé, but compare their intensity with the relatively dilute style of a Touraine Sauvignon. Set up a tasting of French Sauvignons by including with the last three a Bordeaux Blanc. These are not all pure

Sauvignon, so be careful in your selection. Some are labelled as Sauvignon, or ask your merchant. Still high in acidity it will typically be lower than one from the Loire.

For a different view, try one from the list against an oaky Californian Fumé Blanc. Decide for yourself whether or not the oak helps or hinders (there is no correct answer here, just personal opinion).

Gewürztraminer masterclass

Ranges of Gewürztraminer are less widely available than Sauvignon. Try to track down a Central or Eastern European version to compare with the Alsace sample. Try also a range from Alsace. Compare a supermarket own label Gewürztraminer with one from a recognized house, such as Schlumberger, Hugel, Faller or Trimbach, and search out a Grand Cru example for Gewürztraminer at its most sensual and seductive.

04 neutral or delicately flavoured dry white wines

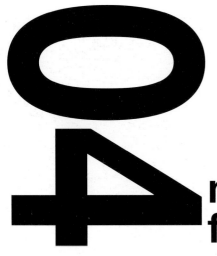

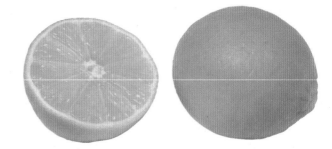

Many, or rather most, white grapes produce delicately flavoured, or even quite neutral wines. Sauvignon Blanc is famous for its almost aggressive pungency, Muscat for its perfume, but not all wines are like that, neither should they be. There is an important market for more delicate flavours, wines that complement simply cooked fish, or fresh salad, or can be drunk unaccompanied as a refreshing and unchallenging aperitif.

No wine should be, or indeed could be, completely tasteless – if it were why not drink water? But neither should all wines be full-flavoured and aromatic. The flavours here are going to be far more subtle than in the previous chapter, identification may be a little more challenging and similes difficult to find. Descriptors like apple, lime, lemon (or just citrus), green fruit, grassy and herbaceous are all used extensively for these wines, as, unfortunately, are terms such as bland, boring, or worse, cardboard, damp earth and drains. Yet the range of wines

made from unaromatic grapes is vast, from wines whose only asset is their inability to cause offence, and wines that make a positive virtue of their neutrality, to some of the finest and most renowned white wines of the world.

The key task for the wine maker is to preserve what little fruit flavours nature has given, within the confines of the marketplace. Volumes are all-important here as elsewhere, so a producer of even the most basic Chablis will charge a higher price than the maker of a basic Frascati, but then is required to pick a smaller quantity of grapes. The two big threats here are poor wine making that results in the unflattering terms like cardboard, and excessive use of cool temperature fermentation, which can mean that the primary fruit flavours are overpowered by confectionary or bubble-gum aromas. It is almost as if the wine maker has to walk a tightrope between being too clean and cutting corners in the hygiene department.

Wines of this style are made all over the world, sometimes, as with the more basic Vin de Tables of France, or bulk-produced Soave, at low prices, and in other cases, such as Chablis or Gavi, at premium price points.

Italy

There can be no doubt that the Italians are masters in the art of producing delicate white wines. As a rule, the Italian taste is for full-flavoured reds but whites are not meant to taste of exotic fruit, of spice, smoke or cats' urine. Wine, it is felt, not unreasonably, should taste vinous – of wine. That is not in any way to say that Italian white wines are uninteresting. There are plenty of examples of high quality dry white Italian wines with great character, but they tend not to be aromatic.

The biggest-selling Italian white is Soave, available from almost every wine shop and supermarket, and probably in every Italian restaurant on the planet. Soave is made from Garganega, blended with two different versions of Trebbiano. Try a basic Soave by all means, but also try something from one of the top producers, like Pieropan, or one of the single 'cru' (i.e. single vineyard) wines that are now available if you search them out. Failing that, go for the Classico designation on the label; this hillier area gives great depth to the wines. Tried against a basic example, the difference is amazing. On the one hand a hopefully clean and correct wine, but one that you cannot get enthusiastic about; on the other wine with great finesse and structure, but yet one that is still difficult to describe. Perhaps a hint of nuts – bitter almonds maybe – perhaps the vaguest hint of tropical fruit, but only a hint. What you will find with the better wine is a great vinosity, a more satisfying mouthfeel than the cheap version.

If you like the style of Soave you will also like wines such as Verdicchio, specifically Verdicchio dei Castelli di Jesi, Frascati and Orvieto Secco – the last two being Trebbianno-based with more or less Malvasia added to the blend. The greater the Malvasia content, the fuller and more interesting the wine. These are the old standards of Italian wine lists, wines that no self-respecting merchant could do without. However, times have changed and today you are more likely to find wines such as Pinot Bianco or Pinot Grigio from one of the most northerly Italian regions like Trentino-Alto Adige or Friuli-Venezia Giulia. Pinot Grigio is, of course, simply Italian for Pinot Gris, but the Italian style is far removed from the lush oily and spicy style of a top Alsace wine. Here the classic Italian style comes through more than the varietal character.

The northern half of Italy is littered with wines that fit into this category. Soave's neighbour, Bianco di Custoza, and the various Tocai wines of Friuli-Venezia Giulia are similar but different, and well worth comparing. In Piemonte the finest still white is Gavi, a DOCG (the highest category in Italian wine law) wine of great finesse albeit with a price to match, made from the Cortese grape. Try a Gavi against a range of other Italian whites. You will certainly find it crisp with very delicate and lime juice hints on the nose, but although fundamentally neutral, it does have a certain elegance that is often lacking in many of its peers. Erbaluce and Arneis are two other Piemontese varieties to look out for.

In Tuscany, the white wine from Trebbiano sold as Galestro is perhaps the ultimate in clean, fresh but neutral wine. Orvieto, from Umbria, south of Tuscany (Toscana) and north of Rome, was once mostly sweetish but the fashion is now for the drier style, making most Orvieto Secco almost indistinguishable from Frascati, from the vineyards just south of Rome.

Most of the best-known wines from southern Italy are red, and many of the new wave of white wines from the south are in the modern, oak influenced style but there is one very widely available variety from the southern Italian island of Sicily. This is Corvo, the branded white wine which manages to be totally acceptable despite being made in such a hot part of the world.

France

Some of the most famous wines of France fit into the unaromatic category. Muscadet, Chablis and Mâcon Blanc, along with the Pinot Blanc and Sylvaner from Alsace, belong here, as do the pure Sémillon dry whites of Bordeaux and many lesser wines from the south of the country.

The Loire is perhaps most famous for wines such as Sancerre that we have already met but it also produces a range of far less pungent wines. The biggest-selling Loire wine in most markets is Muscadet, a wine that combines fresh fruit with relatively low levels of alcohol and marked acidity. It is a wine for hot summer days, meant to accompany seafood at its freshest.

Further inland we get to Anjou, home of Anjou Blanc, a wine that in contrast to the honeyed, concentrated Savennières, demonstrates the range that Chenin is capable of. None of that concentration here, or further upriver, still in Touraine, where Chenin is joined by the local Arbois. Both pleasant enough, but it is easy to understand why Sancerre and Pouilly Fumé from the central vineyards are better known.

Alsace, by way of contrast, makes some far more serious wines even from their less flavoursome grapes. Look out for Alsace Pinot Blanc or Sylvaner. These, from good producers, will yield little on the nose apart from vinousness, but they will have great depth and they form a very satisfying accompaniment to meatier fish dishes.

This extra degree of body and weight is what makes good Chablis too. Chablis comes from around the village of the same name in the most northerly part of Burgundy. (True Chablis comes only from here, but like Champagne, the name has been taken in vain by wine producers and has become a generic term for dry white wines in some parts of the world. This is less so now than in the past, but it still happens.) Here the climate is cool and only the very ripest wines have the fruit and concentration to successfully stand oak ageing, and so most wines labelled as Chablis, and certainly Petit Chablis, are pure Chardonnay without oak. (Premier and Grand Cru wines are increasingly seeing oak fermentation and maturation.) At the other end of Burgundy, just north of Beaujolais, is Mâcon where Chardonnay at the cheaper end of the price range tends to be unoaked. Buy a wine labelled Mâcon Blanc or Mâcon-Villages and compare it to a standard, but fairly young, Chablis. Note the higher acidity of the latter and its flinty, sometimes called steely, character. Green apple fruit is another common descriptor. The Mâcon may have more red apple character, a feature that comes from being grown in slightly warmer climes. The Mâcon will be richer and fuller on the palate with less crisp acidity.

Most Chablis is drunk very young but the higher acidity acts as a preservative so that even the basic versions are capable of maturing and developing for a few years, with the better wines, and in particular the Premier and Grand Cru wines, being capable of ageing for far longer than most people are willing to let them. The richer Mâcon may well seem more appealing at this stage, but because it does not have the acidic backbone of intensity of fruit, it will be best enjoyed fairly young, within two or three years of the vintage. Both wines have the classic unoaked

Chardonnay identity. Chardonnay in its unadorned form is not big, rich and buttery. All those tasting notes come from barrel fermentation and maturation, or from the malo-lactic fermentation.

In Bordeaux the dry whites can be a made from a number of varieties, with Sauvignon and Sémillon dominating. Sémillon has richness and gives the wine a full, sometimes waxy or oily, texture that makes it ideal as a food accompaniment, but this is often blended with Sauvignon for flavour and at the top end oak is often used. You will occasionally still come across a pure unoaked Sémillon but it is difficult to tell from the label what you are going to get in the bottle.

If you are looking for wines in this style without paying Chablis prices, there are plenty of examples from the 'lesser' ACs of southern France, such as white Corbières or almost any white AC wine from Languedoc or Provence. Still further down the price scale are the Vins de Pays from areas such as Gascony – look out for a Colombard Vins de Pays de Gascogne. Many of the white Vins de Pays from Languedoc-Roussillon today are made from international varieties such as Chardonnay or Viognier and tend to be either aromatic or oaky.

Spain

It is one of the great paradoxes of wine development that the parts of the world that have hot climates produce the best full-bodied red wines, while the areas with less sun and cooler conditions make the best whites. Unfortunate because regions in hot areas have a far greater thirst for refreshing, chilled dry whites. Spain makes plenty of good reds, but the native white grapes generally are far from exciting. Viura, the grape that makes white Rioja and, as Macabeo, is part of the Cava blend is an exception, but Airen, the most important grape in Spain, and indeed the most widely planted grape in the world, competes for the title of the most boring grape on the planet. One of its competitors is Listan, known in Spain as Palomino. The grape of Sherry, it produces the most unexciting of light wines. There are other good white grapes too, like Verdejo in Rueda, but in this hot and dry country there is still an uncomfortably large volume of thoroughly boring white wine.

La Mancha, the arid plain of central Spain, produces millions of hectolitres of simple, everyday wine that is now perfectly drinkable – far better than it once was – but generally there is little more positive that one can say about it. Valencia, a little to the east, also makes wine that the retail buyers use for basic house wine or cheap special offers. Of more interest are the wines of Rueda, further north. Much of the production is now made as a blend of Verdejo with Sauvignon Blanc to add some aromatics, just as the Bordeaux producers add Sauvignon to their Sémillon.

Viura in Rioja is often seen in its oaked form, but there are unoaked white Riojas around too. Look for one that has no indication of ageing on the back label – avoid even a Crianza for this. Note the vinousity of the wine, a rich palate that comes from ripe grapes, but very little in terms of varietal character.

Portugal

Most of the best Portuguese whites are mildly aromatic – more so than the Spanish or Italian whites. Increasingly Portuguese white wine is made in a modern oak-flavoured style. Vinho Verde at its best has more character than the majority of Muscadet, and has a similar high acid/low alcohol profile. For the most part the Vinho Verde that is exported is slightly sweetened for commercial reasons.

In the classic neutral mould are wines such as Bucellas from near Lisbon, and the white wines of Dão, Bairrada and the Douro. These were, until very recently, mostly sold far too old, often oxidized and tasting flat. Things have moved on and you will get far cleaner, fresher wines, but the reds are generally more satisfying.

Germany

As a contrast to hot countries that tend to make good reds and unexciting whites, cool regions – where a warming high-alcohol red would be most welcome – are past masters at flavoursome white wines. Think of Germany and you think of Riesling. But another very traditional German grape is Silvaner – note the change of spelling here from Alsace, the German authorities are very strict on that. Most German regions have some Silvaner but look out for one from Franken, preferably labelled 'trocken', which means dry. Franken wines are bottled in the distinctive Bocksbeutel, the same bottle that Sogrape of Portugal chose for Mateus Rosé – to the long-term chagrin of the Franconians.

Austria

Staying in a German-speaking country, try an Austrian Grüner Veltliner. This is a native of Austria, of which very little ever is grown anywhere else. Grüner Veltliner's character is delicate and very subtle. Flavour profiles include lime and other citrus and spice, but very delicately spiced. Austria uses similar labelling terms to Germany, so choose a Qualitätswein for this. Note the similarity to a young Chablis in both flavour and structure – dry, crisp acidity and light flavour yet with a good length and quite satisfying. Austrian wine makers tend to make wine that is either totally dry, far drier than many others labelled dry, or fully sweet, with very little in between.

New World

The New World countries are most famous for their big, bold, full-flavoured and full-bodied wines. However, there are a number of exceptions. All countries make a considerable volume of unoaked, less full wines, and we are increasingly seeing unoaked Chardonnays from Australia, and less expensive dry whites from California.

Pre-eminent among the New World producers of this style of wine, though, has to be South Africa. For many years South Africa found it difficult to export her wine, so the growers catered for the local market, which wanted undemanding, refreshing dry white wines to drink by the poolside or with the 'braai' (barbecue). As a result the most important grape grown, in what should be mainly a red-wine-producing country, is Chenin Blanc. Alongside this there are acres of Colombard, another neutral variety that is good for Brandy production. Compare a South African Chenin to one from Anjou. Perhaps the southern hemisphere version will be a little riper, perhaps less acid, but they share very much the same character.

Uses for more delicate wines

It is very easy to dismiss delicate wines in blind tastings because they do not jump out of the glass and identify themselves. This is unfortunate as they are in many ways the most versatile of white wines, with flavours that do not overpower food. Drink them as an aperitif or with lightly flavoured dishes and salads.

5 oak influenced white wines

Part of the popularity of wine is mystique. Rightly or wrongly we are all seduced by the image that wine portrays, and a large part of that is the dark, arched-roofed, low-ceilinged cellars filled with cobweb-covered barrels. Wherever wine is made, the image persists; wine and barrels are indivisibly linked. Even in the most modern industrial-scale wineries, those in which millions of gallons of wine are made in stainless steel tanks, there will be a small sack of barriques in the visitors' centre to help maintain the tradition.

This romantic view of wine making is no longer accurate but the wine drinker's love affair with oak remains strong, so much so that many back and even front labels boast of oak maturation – the only vinificational technique afforded such an accolade.

Oak casks of one form or another have been the storage vessels of choice for the wine maker since the progression from using goatskins. Until relatively recently there was no other choice: stainless steel, glass-reinforced plastic (fibreglass) and concrete were only introduced into the winery in the twentieth century, so all wine stored in bulk was stored in oak. Other woods have been used, chestnut is still found occasionally, but the overwhelming preference has been for oak beloved of the coopers and wine makers. Easy to work, it imparts a pleasant flavour when new, but can continue to be used for storage years after the smoky, vanilla flavours of new wood have been absorbed by previous vintages.

Why use oak?

Wood has two main effects: one is simply flavouring the wine, where components in the wood dissolve in the wine, giving it the now familiar smoky, vanilla or fresh cut wood smell. The other is more subtle, an interaction between liquid with the wood resulting in a slow oxidative ageing through the large surface area of wood in contact with the wine. This, not oak flavour, is the really important characteristic of oak, the reason that so many of the world's finest wines have spent time in oak. Oak offers extra roundness, generosity of body and fullness on the palate, as well as a touch of extra complexity.

The effect varies depending on the size and age of the vessel concerned – in new casks, how the wood has been cut, and on the 'toast' the cooper has applied when curving and shaping the staves. Oak can be sawn or split, the former allowing it to release more flavour more rapidly into the wine, and the wine maker will specify high, medium or light toasting – i.e. firing – when placing their order with the cooper.

What's more, different forests give different oaks, leading to great variety. The vast wooden vats seen in some Portuguese and Italian wineries are so large and the wood so old that no oak flavour remains. Add to that the generous layer of tartrate crystals invariably found lining the vat and it soon becomes apparent that no flavour pick-up is possible. At the other end of the scale are the new, heavily charred – 'high toast' – new American oak barrique, a mere 225 litres in capacity, giving a high ratio

Barrel fermentation will normally be followed by a period of maturation in the cask, frequently with 'lees stirring', or 'battonage'. This adds still greater complexity as the yeast gives richness and creaminess to the wine.

Barrel fermentation is almost exclusively a white wine technique; no wine maker wants grape skins, essential for extraction of colour, in the barrel. There are, however, an increasing number of red wines ending their fermentation, after pressing, in the same casks that they will subsequently be matured in.

Oak maturation

Wines fermented in inert vessels, stainless steel or glass-lined concrete, can still benefit from a period of new wood maturation before bottling. Look for 'cask' or 'barrel matured' on the label. These wines are normally less intensely oaky than their barrel-fermented cousins, but again the wine has to be good to stand the oak ageing. There is also a view, widely held among wine makers, that barrel fermentation results in a more integrated whole than just maturation.

cooperage is a highly-skilled occupation
here a cooper reshapes a stave while repairing a cask

of wood to wine, and therefore greater depth and intensity of flavour.

... and when?

Barrel fermentation

Oak can be used for both fermentation and storage vessels. For the fullest oak flavour look out for a Californian or Australian Chardonnay with the words 'barrel fermented' on the label. The action of fermentation draws more of the vanillin flavour and tannins out of the wood. Barrel fermentation is expensive. Not only does the wine maker have to buy the barrel (currently around £400 each for French oak), the work involved in using casks of 225 litres (barriques) or 300 litres is significantly higher than fermenting in bulk tanks. Expect to pay a premium price for a genuine barrel-fermented wine, but only the best musts will be used, so it should still represent good value.

must being pumped into new oak casks for barrel fermentation
new oak gives the greatest degree of oak flavour

Some wines that spend time in oak get little or no flavour directly from the wood. Rather, they soften and gain complexity through the minutely slow ingress of oxygen through the pores of the wood, the sides of the bung and the inevitable aeration during racking (see Chapter 16).

When 'oak' does not mean 'cask'

It has long been recognized by the makers of fine wines that a period of oak maturation softens tannins in red wines and adds complexity and texture to white wines, while the acidity is reduced, partly through malo-lactic fermentation, and partly through the general softening effect of the wood. Where used, new wood has always been reserved for the finest wines, with second, third and subsequent fillings generally being with lesser wine. As a result the flavour of new wood came to be associated with fine wine, even though the traditional view was that the wine would subsequently need time to mature in the bottle, to allow wood flavours to integrate with the fruit flavours of wine. Many of today's oaky wines have never been anywhere near a cask. The oak flavour comes from adding oak chips or powder, or suspending planks of oak in the wine while it ferments or matures in a stainless steel vat. To some this is cheating; to others it is simply satisfying customer demand. Either way, the technique is here to stay, even though it is banned for AC wine in France, and by similar laws in other EU countries. Outside the strict confines of the quality wine regimes it is not only permitted but widely practised, so expect your cheap Vin de Pays d'Oc Chardonnay to have seen oak chips, not barrels.

Grapes that like oak, grapes that don't

Wines made from aromatic grapes will not tend to see oak, or if they do, it will be old oak that does not add superfluous flavours to the wine. Look around any traditional Alsatian or German cellar and you will find plenty of oak. But look again, this is not new wood. Old wood that has long since lost its oaky flavours is preferred here. Look more closely still and you will see that some of the casks are commemorative – Schloss Johannisberg's phylloxera cask, or Hugel's 200-year-old St Catherine cask are clearly not replaced every vintage – indeed as long as the wood remains clean and sweet, these casks will be maintained and used.

old wood does not input any oaky flavour but does have a role to play in maturation

Neither will you find oak in the simple everyday drinks consumed in vast quantities all over the southern part of Europe. The cost of adding oak flavours, by whatever means, is just not justified.

Other grapes have a natural affinity for oak. Chardonnay is the most classic example of this, but many other grapes yield wines that, while fairly neutral, are well structured and benefit from the extra flavours. Sémillon is another grape that, like Chardonnay, has very little flavour as such, but does have a great breadth on the palate, a texture rather than a flavour. Wine makers in both Bordeaux and Australia, Sémillon's two most important homes, give it the barrel fermentation treatment.

The Spanish have always had a love affair with oak, particularly the cheaper, and more powerfully oaky American oak. Rioja especially makes white wines that have been subjected to long oak ageing. The style of oak aged Rioja has been changing of late, with only one or two producers, most famously Murrieta and La Rioja Alta, keeping to the traditional, slightly oxidative style, with the rest preferring a more reductive, fruit-driven style, with shorter oak maturation.

Increasingly you will find all sorts of different varieties being given the kiss of oak – sometimes successfully, other times not. There have been some very successful German Silvaners (Sylvaners) for example, where again the mouthfeel of the grape, rather than its perfume, is important.

However, although oak fermented or aged aromatic varieties must fill a need, the oak often seems at odds with the fruit. Sauvignon and Viognier surely have enough character to survive on their own.

The taste of oak

There will be plenty of opportunities to taste oak in many other wines, so this exercise is designed to illustrate exactly what oak tastes of.

Start off with two Chardonnays, one with oak and one without. You could use Burgundies here, with a Chablis and wine from the Côte d'Or, but in order to keep costs down, you could choose from almost anywhere in the world these days. Ideally you should have wines from the same or a similar region, so the climate is not a variable. Australia, California, South Africa and Spain all produce suitable pairings that are reasonably widely available.

Select one wine that boasts about barrel fermentation on the label, and the other that doesn't mention oak at all. (Increasingly, as fashions change there is a move to boasting about wine being 'unoaked' which makes our choice easier.)

Looking at the two samples you will immediately see that the oaked wine is deeper in colour, with a golden hue rather than the lemon yellow of the unoaked version.

On the nose the difference becomes even more apparent. Smell the unoaked wine first. It should be clean, fresh, and have notes of lemon, perhaps peach and apricots if from a warm climate, green apples if from a cool one. The palate is likely to be fresh again, dry, crisp in acidity wherever it is from, with a medium body. Note the breadth of the palate, though, while you taste it.

The barrel-fermented wine will smell of vanilla, biscuits, butterscotch or timber yard, maybe smoky, all overlaying the fruit, which is likely to be riper – perhaps melon or tropical fruit coming through if the wine originates from somewhere hot. Depending on how the wine has been made, you may well find creamy characters too. The palate will feel fuller, the extra weight being in the main the result of the wood.

To see how this compares with the taste of oak chips, add a cheaper wine to the tasting. Buy a bottle of inexpensive Vin de Pays Chardonnay, or branded Australian Chardonnay. Read the label carefully. You are looking for the implication of wood, without the word barrel, or barrique, or any other true oak vessel appearing. Something that says 'the fruit is complemented by subtle hints of oak' would be ideal. This invariably means chips have been used. Note how the wine smells just as oaky as the last, but probably has less fruit. This is because the wines that are 'chipped' are generally the lesser wines, it is not because of the chips. The wine will probably have less body for the same reason. It will certainly have more

youthful, primary fruit because it will never have been exposed to the slight aeration that is an inevitable consequence of using real barrels. What you might or might not detect is a slight bitterness in the back of the throat that can come from the use of oak chips.

Having tried a range of fruit-driven wines with oak, try one of the really traditional Riojas. The difference here is oxidation, which comes across as a depression of the primary fruit flavours, and an extra nuttiness on the nose. Sometimes people refer to this as Sherry-like. Oxidation when the wine maker does not want it is a fault, but in certain wines, such as old-fashioned Rioja, it is kept under control and is a vital part of the wine's style.

medium white wines

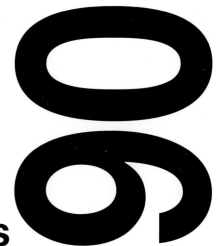

We all start our wine-drinking careers with something a little sweet. In the 1970s and 1980s wines such as Liebfraumilch, Niersteiner Gutes Domtal and Piesporter Michelsberg were the weaning wines. In the 1990s, they gave way to Lambrusco, itself followed by cheap Australian Chardonnay or a Californian 'jug' wine as the beginners' wines of choice. These wines all have one thing in common – they are totally inoffensive because they are sweetish.

Wine is an alien flavour to most of us when we start to drink it, and anything too strong in flavour, or too structured, is seen as harsh, sour or aggressive. As beginners, we are drawn to the softness that sweetness brings, to the obvious fruitiness that these wines have and to the price. Generally these are among the cheapest wines on the shelf.

As time goes on, we move on, developing our tastes, experimenting with different wine styles and gradually finding new wines we like. Usually the progression is towards the drier end of the spectrum. All too often, we then leave the medium-dry wines alone, with all too few of us returning to the medium style. I am not suggesting we go back to the Piesporters of our youth, but to discover the truly glorious flavours that are available from wines such as a Rheingau Auslese or a demi-sec Vouvray. There is a world of difference between the cheap, sugary, bland wine sold as Piesporter Michelsberg Quälitatswein and a Piesporter Goldtröpfchen Kabinett.

'Medium' is a little difficult to define. Most wines are naturally dry, others, such as Sauternes and Tokay, are definitely sweet. Between these extremes are the medium wines, but descriptions will vary from off-dry through medium dry to medium sweet. Some retailers, led by the now defunct Wine Promotion Board, have tried to define sweetness by number using a scale of 1 to 9 scale where 1 represents the driest and 9 the sweetest. This helps, but personal taste is more important. The same wine might be described by one taster as medium sweet and by another as medium dry. In this chapter we will look at the range from medium dry to medium sweet, leaving the fully sweet wines for the next chapter.

Achieving medium-ness

Medium-dry wines are made in a number of different ways and all include arrested fermentation in some way. Any sweetness in a still wine must be grape sugar – it is forbidden to sweeten by adding cane or beet sugars. (Note the difference here between still and sparkling wine.) Before World War II it was very difficult to make stable wines with this level of residual sugar; paradoxically, fully sweet wines are naturally more stable than those with lower levels of sweetness. In the latter half of the twentieth century filtration techniques were developed that made it possible to remove yeast and bacteria. The German wine industry in particular took to this in a big way and made a whole range of sweet and semi-sweet wines. Prior to this some vats might stop fermenting naturally but this was the exception rather than the rule.

Such wines still happen occasionally, and there are a handful of producers who will allow the wine itself to dictate its final style – if it ferments to dryness it will be sold as such, if fermentation stops prematurely it will be sold as medium. More common is the arresting of fermentation by sterile filtration. Many medium-dry wines from the Loire are made this way.

A still more common method is the addition of a grape must as a sweetener. This technique involves removing a small amount of must from the press, which is not allowed to ferment; it is usually filtered, dosed with sulphur dioxide and kept refrigerated. This is blended back into the wine just before bottling. This technique, known in Germany as Süssreserve and in Australia as back-blending, is probably the most widely used. This is not concentrated grape sugar, as used in sweetening pale cream Sherry, simply unfermented must.

In Germany the addition of Süssreserve is strictly controlled so that the sweetening is of the same quality as the base wine to which it is being added. For example, if a wine maker is sweetening a Spätlese, the Süssreserve too must be of Spätlese quality. In theory it can be added to any quality level, although in practice the fully sweet Beerenauslesen and Trockenbeerenauslesens will not need it.

Why make medium wines?

The addition or retention of a little sweetening is particularly important for wines that are high in acidity but which are likely to be consumed on their own. In Germany wine is seen as a beverage in its own right, rather than a part of the meal. Fully dry wines would taste austere and the acidity naturally present in these wines, especially those made from Riesling, needs this touch of balance.

Vinho Verde producers use the same argument. As we saw in Chapter 4, Vinho Verde sold in Portugal is dry but the major export brands are slightly sweetened to balance the high acidity. Truly dry Vinho Verde is quite delicious with fresh fish on Portugal's Atlantic coast, but seems very tart in cooler climates.

Wines of all colours, made specifically for inexperienced wine drinkers, are often sweetened too. Branded French wines such as Piat d'Or (red and white), which is made specifically for the UK market, and the world famous Mateus and Lancers brands of rosé are medium. New wine consumers are reassured by a brand they recognize, and they like the taste.

All of this sounds apologetic; it is not necessarily so. The top medium-dry wines are not a second best – they can be among the finest and most useful wines on the list. No wine lover who has tasted the great Rieslings of Wiltingen or Wehlen could ever deny their quality. The racy acidity and elegance of fruit means these wines are unparalleled among white wines.

Most of us reach for a dry wine to accompany food, but a great deal of modern cooking involves sugar in some form or another. Look at any modern cookery book, particularly one that includes oriental or 'fusion' cuisine, and you will find sugar added either directly or through sweet vegetables and fruit. Such dishes demand a touch of sweetness in the wine.

Tasting medium wines

Germany

As Germany is the most famous producer of this style of wine we will start there. Germany has a cool climate that makes grape ripening a challenge. As a result of this, the German wine law is different from the rest of Europe. In France and Italy it is the provenance that matters, the difference between Villages and Grand Cru level, or between normale and classico. It is nothing more or less than where the grapes were grown. A vins de table vineyard can only make vins de table. In Germany it is the ripeness of the grapes at harvest time that matters. All German vineyards are capable of making all qualities of wine, from the most basic Deutscher Tafelwein to the highest grades of quality wine, depending on the vintage.

Like all European Union wine producers, Germany has two grades of wine, table wine, labelled either Deutscher Tafelwein or Deutscher Landwein, and quality wine, labelled Qualitätswein, divided into Qualitätswein bestimmter Angaugebiete (QbA, but often simple labelled Qualitätswein) and Qualitätswein mit Prädikat (QmP), the latter being further subdivided into six different Prädikat levels. The difference between

Qualitätswein bestimmter Angaugebiete and Qualitätswein mit Prädikat is that QmP wines are not chaptalized (the addition of sugar to grape must before fermentation to increase the final alcohol strength). The alcohol is entirely a result of the fermentation of the naturally occurring grape sugars. See Chapter 16.

The full list of German wine categories is:

- Deutscher Tafelwein
- Deutscher Landwein
- Qualitätswein bestimmter Angaugebiete
- Qualitätswein mit Prädikat
- Kabinett (grapes harvested at the normal time, but more ripe than those for QbA)
- Spätlese (late harvest – riper grapes as a result of longer time on the vine)
- Auslese (selected bunches of the ripest grapes)
- Beerenauslese (selected berries or parts of bunches – usually affected by noble rot)
- Eiswein (grapes picked and pressed while frozen – the freezing concentrates the juice if the frozen pulp is discarded)
- Trockenbeerenauslese (selected individual grape berries, very ripe and shrivelled by noble rot).

Landwein must be either trocken (dry) or halbtrocken (literally half, or medium dry, but is in fact drier than most German wines drunk in the UK and can therefore be left out of this chapter). Equally the top grapes of Qualitätswein mit Prädikat, the Beerenauslesen, Eiswein and Trockenbeerenauslesen are dessert wines, which we will look at in the next chapter. Here we will look at QbA and the lower levels of QmP.

QbA tasting

It is instructive to remind ourselves of where we came from so for this first exercise, compare a cheap Liebfraumilch or Niersteiner Gutes Domtal with a QbA Riesling. Pay a little more for the latter, but for this tasting it does not need to be expensive. Avoid wine labelled trocken or classic, which will be too dry to make a fair comparison.

Taste the cheaper wine first. It doesn't state a grape variety so it is almost certainly going to be made predominantly from Müller-Thurgau, a grape developed in the nineteenth century. At best it gives clean, fairly aromatic floral wines, and if you are lucky yours might be like that. It is more likely to be dull, overly sulphurous, and smell of damp cardboard. On the palate it will be medium dry to medium sweet, depending on the example you choose, with balanced acidity at best. Don't forget that wines like this still make up a remarkably large part of the wine market.

The Riesling will be far fresher, with much clearer fruit, lively floral or citrus aromas, and possibly a touch of wax or oil on the nose too. The palate, too, will be far fresher with that fine racy acidity that is a hallmark of fine Riesling, and a far longer finish.

QmP tasting

Having looked at the basic qualities, compare them to the first levels of QmP. Staying with Riesling, compare a Kabinett with a Spätlese. Choose wines from the same region. The Mosel is an ideal starting point. Get hold of an example of each quality grade, preferably from the same vintage. Look out for both the region – always given in full of the label as Mosel-Saar-Ruhr – and the grape variety, for this exercise it needs to be Riesling. Again, as we are looking at medium wines, avoid trockens.

Notice how the purity of fruit flavour that you noticed in the QbA is even greater here, with a wonderful delicacy of touch yet at the same time an intensity of flavour. Did you notice the alcohol? Typically only 7.5 to 8.5 per cent in the Kabinett and yet still perfectly balanced.

Comparing the two, you may or may not find that the Spätlese is sweeter. It is tempting to assume that late harvest wines are going to be sweeter, but it all depends on when the fermentation is stopped, so a Spätlese can be either sweeter or higher in alcohol. What you will certainly find is great weight and intensity of flavour, with perhaps more honeyed notes to the nose, and far greater intensity.

If you compared it to an Auslese the differences would be correspondingly greater, with most Auslesen being sweeter still. It is possible, however, to ferment any of these three, Kabinett, Spätlese and Auslese, to dryness, with a corresponding increase in alcohol.

Regional differences

Most of us are familiar with French regions and we would not tend to group the Rhône with the Loire, or Alsace with Languedoc, yet we do not tend to see

Germany as separate regions, but as one. To experience a little of the flavour of different regions compare the Kabinett that you just tried with one from the Pfalz.

The Mosel is in the north of the vine-growing area of Germany, the Pfalz is considerably further south and is protected by the Harz mountains, which is the same range of mountains as the Vosges that protect Alsace. The grapes are therefore riper here, with greater concentration of both sugar and flavour.

The Mosel wine should be crisp, with a fruity, citrus flavour, perhaps lime and lemon, developing into oil or wax with age. The Pfalz example is likely to be more melon or peach flavoured, sweeter fruit, with a fuller body, although not exactly full bodied in the overall scale of things.

France

Much French medium wine is at the cheap end of the market, branded table wines that try to compete with Liebfraumilch. There are, however, a number of really stunning medium wines made in Alsace and the Loire.

We have already come across the main grapes of Alsace in the dry white wine sections, but many producers are making their Gewürztraminers and Pinot Gris in a slightly sweet style. This of course matches the rich aromatic flavours of the wines.

The Loire's medium wines are mostly made from Chenin Blanc. Appellations such as Vouvray and Montlouis in Touraine are the classics. Savannières in Anjou is usually dry but there are exceptions in particularly good vintages or from exceptional sites. The wines of Côteaux du

springtime in the gently rolling vineyards of the Pfalz

Layon are medium sweet rather than medium dry, and we will look at those in the next chapter.

The easiest of these to get hold of is Vouvray, from vineyards north of the river Loire, just up river from the city of Tours. Confusingly, many producers do not always put the style of wine on the label, so you will need to speak to the retailer to ensure you get a medium wine.

When you take it, think about the German Riesling. The nose will perhaps be a little more honeyed, perfumed, and even musky. Descriptors can be difficult for Chenin because of the variations in both intensity and flavour but they can include floral, wax, lanolin and even wet dog or damp tweed jacket, but the aromatic character can remind people of Riesling despite this. On the palate the high natural acidity is almost Riesling-like, but typically a medium Vouvray will be higher in alcohol for any given sweetness level.

Montlouis, just across the river from Vouvray, produces very similar wines to its more famous northern neighbour. Perhaps a little lighter in style, it suffers from being far less well known outside the area, but that means it tends to be better value if you do see it.

Italy

Italy produces a vast range of medium wines, most famously perhaps Lambrusco Bianco, made for the export markets only – the version drunk in Italy is red. Lambrusco is a frizzante wine, semi-sparkling, a common style in many parts of the country. Similar and far better wines are made in Veneto from the vaguely aromatic Prosecco, and in Piemonte from Moscato. The latter are available as basic table wines or the delicious Moscato d'Asti, the semi-sparkling and lower alcohol version of the more famous Asti sparkling wine.

Rest of the world

Inexpensive wines from California and Australia are often made in this style, both for their domestic markets and the cheaper wines for export. The touch of residual sugar makes basic Chardonnays popular.

In South Africa the word 'steen' on the label indicates a Chenin Blanc made in an odd dry to medium style.

At higher price points and quality levels many countries produce Rieslings in a medium style as well as dry. Compare an Eden Valley Riesling from Australia, and a New Zealand one with one from Germany. Note the extra weight in the southern hemisphere versions, and the more citrus-like, lime juice in particular, flavours.

Medium white wines with food

Many medium white wines are designed to be drunk on their own, but don't dismiss them as food accompaniments. Try a Riesling with Chinese food – the combination of sweetness and acidity works perfectly with the sweet and sour flavours of the food and the intensity of fruit works better than many more neutral grapes.

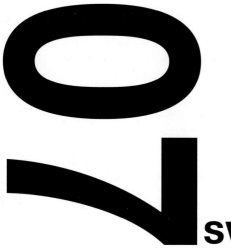

sweet wines

Dessert wines, pudding wines, sweeties; whatever they are called, sweet wines go through ups and downs due to the vagaries of fashion. Today things look healthier for the producers than they did a decade or two ago, but the prices achieved are still far below those of equivalent quality in dry red wines – especially when you consider how low the yields are in comparison. True, the greatest of them all, wines such as Château d'Yquem, and the finest German Eisweins and Trockenbeerenauslesen, are expensive but there are many wines almost as good, but not as famous, that are the real bargains of the wine world.

One of the biggest difficulties facing the sweet wine maker is modern eating habits. Once sweet foods and drinks were prized above all others. Sugar was a luxury and could not be added without thought as it can today, so consumers would pay a premium for anything sweet.

The modern media bombard us with the message that sweet is bad. It seems half the western world is on a diet, so pudding, in the traditional sense, is omitted from the repertoire, replaced on all but the most grand occasions with fresh fruit or a pot of yoghurt. As a result, sweet wines tend to get left on the shelf. So strong is the perceived propaganda against sweetness, and so heartfelt the desire to be seen to be saying the right thing, or perhaps so strong are the memories of cheap, over-sulphured sweet wines at college, that in any consumer tasting group there is always a sizeable contingent who claim not to like sweet wine. When pressed, the same people will often admit to liking Port (sweet but higher in alcohol), and usually the most popular wine in any line-up, the one everyone comes back for seconds of, is the dessert wine.

Sweet wine is far more versatile, though. It is not just for the pudding. The Bordelais and their neighbours in the Dordogne never tire of pointing out that the ideal accompaniment to Sauternes or Montbazillac is foie gras. That it certainly is, but how often do most of us eat foie gras? By the same token, the richness of the wine does complement many other, similarly rich foods. Try Sauternes with a soft, creamy blue cheese such as St Agur or Roquefort, or with a smooth liver pâté – it often works better than a red.

Achieving sweetness

Whereas medium wines are often the result of artificially stopped fermentation, the best sweet wines are made when the fermentation stops naturally, either because the alcohol reaches a level at which the yeast dies, or because the must is too concentrated to allow the yeast to work efficiently. Some sweet wines are made by arresting the fermentation, but the grapes must be far riper than those for medium-dry wines if they are to have a reasonable level of both sweetness and alcohol.

Noble rot, *Botrytis cinerea*

This concentration is usually a severe fungal attack, naturally occurring in certain vineyards in some vintages.

In certain circumstances, when white grapes are ripe, a normally malevolent fungus called *Botrytis cinerea* can attack grapes in a benevolent manner, softening the skin without splitting it and allowing some of the water within the grape berry to evaporate and thereby concentrate the sugar content.

Botrytis thrives in humid conditions. For it to become beneficial, when it is called noble rot, the vineyard should ideally have damp, misty mornings followed by warm, sunny afternoons in the weeks preceding harvest. The mist encourages the fungus; the sun concentrates the grapes. The result is grapes that gradually turn from yellow-green to brown and ultimately purple-brown, shrivelled like raisins but covered in a furry coat of fungus. They look atrocious, but the resulting wine, golden in colour, honeyed, waxy and sweet is delicious.

Noble rot is unpredictable. Some years it will occur reasonably evenly with all grapes succumbing to the fungus. In other years, if weather stays too dry, the grower waits in vain for its arrival. (Sometimes the weather is dry enough to concentrate the grapes, but the essential character of *Botrytis* is missing. In other vintages the autumn rains come too soon, turning the noble rot to grey rot, and a vintage might be written off.)

Usually not all the grapes are affected; it is not an even spread. Some grapes will be suitably shrivelled while others, even on the same bunch, might still be green and healthy. Hand picking is therefore vital; only the ripest, rottenest grapes will be picked with each successive trawl through the vineyard, the rest will be left for another day. The most famous Sauternes château, Château d'Yquem, has been known to have up to a dozen passes through the vines, sometimes without ever making a drop of the famous wine from the results, if the quality isn't there.

Frozen grapes

The concentrating effect of *Botrytis* can also occur with extreme cold. When a solution of water starts to freeze, it is the water that freezes first, so the remaining solution becomes progressively more concentrated. If grapes are subjected to a temperature of about −8 Celsius, for about eight hours, they will freeze, or partially freeze. This is a big risk – the first appropriate frosts might not arrive until well into the January following the main harvest, by which time the grapes might have gone rotten, or been eaten by birds or other pests. It is far safer to pick the

grapes at the normal time – the yields are more reliable, and vastly higher too.

Harvesting is no picnic at the best of times, but being woken in the early hours of the morning to go out to hand pick grapes in temperatures well below freezing must take a particular type of picker. The harvest has to be picked the first time the grapes freeze as allowing the grapes to thaw out again makes the exercise pointless.

The concentrated must struggles to ferment to nine or 10 per cent alcohol, so these tend to be sweeter than many other sweet wines. The freezing not only concentrates the sugar, it also concentrates the acid to a greater extent than with *Botrytis*, so although Eiswein is sweeter, it sometimes does not seem so. This acid also enables the best wines to mature for decades.

Grape drying

If rot and cold can concentrate grape sugars, then so can simple drying. Some of the most historic sweet fortified wines, such as the Cypriot Commandaria, are made from raisined grapes, but there are a number of light wines made this way too, most notably in Italy.

Fortification

Yeast stops working at about 15 per cent vol, so if a wine maker raises the alcohol level over this by simply adding spirit, a stable sweet wine will result. Some wines that are often thought of as normal dessert wines, such as the Muscat-based VDN wines of southern France, are fortified. We will look at this further in Chapter 11.

Tasting quality in sweet wine

Many students of wine claim to dislike sweet wine, yet if you speak to people who have conducted consumer tastings they will all tell you that the sweetie left until the end, after the dry white and reds, will always be the most popular of the flight. The reason is simple: we all like sweet tastes, even if we don't like to admit it, but there is so much cheap, and nasty, sweet wine made that people are put off buying more expensive versions.

We saw in Chapter 1 how acid and sugar balance each other on the palate. Good sweet wine will always have a crisp balancing acidity, which you may not even notice, but which will clean the palate, giving a fresh, lively finish. It would be nice to think that the days of nasty 'Spanish sweet white' selling in every corner off-licence or supermarket have gone, but they have not. If you want to remind yourself how bad the balance is, buy one of these as a reference point for the rest of the chapter. Choose the cheapest you can, preferably a vino da mesa, basic table wine, version. Do not use a wine from Valencia for this, it is likely to be too good.

Compare this with a good quality wine from Sauternes or Barsac. These two appellations, just up river from the city of Bordeaux, are the most famous of all sweet wine areas in France. Here the Sémillon is concentrated by noble rot – *porriture noble* in French – and the balance is achieved by judicious additions of Sauvignon Blanc. Barsac, by the way, is within the Sauternes appellation, so the wines made here have a choice of name. Sauternes should never be cheap – if you find a very cheap example treat it with suspicion, but it is good value, so go for a single château example, preferably a cru classée if you want to splash out.

The wine should look inviting. Wines of this type have a glorious golden lustre in the glass, clinging to the glass as you move it around, a combination of both high alcohol and residual sugar. Smell the wine. Note the honeyed, floral, marmalade characters, richness, sometimes even dustiness on the nose. This is the effect of noble rot. Many of the best Sauternes are aged in new wood, but only rarely does this show through as the concentration of other flavours is so great.

The palate is of course sweet, with a mouth-filling lusciousness that comes in part from the high sugar level, but also from the effect of *Botrytis*. A simple sugar solution of the same concentration would not have the same mouthfeel. The acidity may not be noticeable at all initially, but think about the finish. It will be clean and the saliva glands will be working overtime for quite a while after you have swallowed, a sure sign that the acidity is higher than first impressions indicate.

Other noble rot wines

Around the famous areas of Sauternes and Barsac there is a handful of less well-known appellations making similar wines that are usually less concentrated but represent excellent value. Look out for St Croix du Mont, Cadillac and Loupiac in particular. Further inland,

in the Dordogne, is Monbazillac, again with the same grapes made in a similar style.

We have seen that the Loire makes a range of sweetness levels, with the Chenin Blanc being the ideal grape here. For a real bargain in sweet wines look out for Côteaux du Layon. The Layon is a tributary of the Loire where *Botrytis* affects the Chenin. Côteaux du Layon will tend to be medium sweet to sweet, but with higher acidity than the wine from in and around Bordeaux. In the same valley are the two sweeter and finer areas of Bonnezeaux and Quarts-de-Chaume – both also well worth looking out for, although they are rarer.

On the border between France and Germany the Alsace region produces very fine sweet wines. Look for Sélèction des Grains Nobles for the sweetest, and expect everything we have seen so far from Alsace with a vengeance, along with sweetness.

Wines made from botrytized grapes are highly prized in Germany too. Riesling's ability to continue to develop flavours long after lesser grapes would have stopped, coupled with its high natural acidity, makes it the ideal candidate for sweet wines. As we saw in the previous chapter, the grades of QmP, Beerenauslese and Trockenbeerenauslese are made from rotted berries, with Trockenbeerenauslese, sometimes abbreviated to TBA, being the most concentrated.

The temperatures in German cellars tend to be lower than those in more southern countries, especially as the harvest is later, so the yeast finds it even more difficult to work. The result is that many German sweet wines are very low in alcohol, 8 or 9 per cent is not unusual. This means the wines tend to be a little sweeter than a French equivalent picked at the same grape-sugar level, but the racy acidity makes for a lighter, less unctuous palate. These are well worth trying, but be warned. Whereas the prices for Sauternes are generally lower than you might expect given the provenance and ridiculously low yields, the price asked for the finest German sweet wines is well outside the pocket-money bracket. Hardly surprising given the effort that goes into making them.

Hungary's legendary Tokay wines are also made from *Botrytis*-affected berries, but are handled differently. There are a number of different Tokay wines, but here we are most concerned with Tokay Aszú, Aszú being the Hungarian term for botrytized berries.

The other wines we have looked at here are made from rotten berries, possibly with a proportion of unaffected berries included in the mix. In the case of Tokay Aszú, however, the heavily botritic berries are kept separate from the unaffected ones. The healthy berries are turned into either must or wine and then the rotten berries added. The proportion added was traditionally measured in *puttony*, so the higher the *puttonyos* figure quoted on the label, the sweeter the finished wine.

During the communist period all Tokay came from the central cellars, but now there are a number of independent producers, each making a slightly different style of wine, just as there are in most other regions of the world. What you will find, though, is a deeper colour than you have come across in the other sweet wines, with the marmalade and honey character often joined by caramel or toffee. Tokay Aszú is usually sold in 50 cl clear glass, dumpy bottles. It is one of the world's classic wines and is well worth looking out for.

Eiswein

Eiswein production is inevitably restricted to certain parts of the world. Germany and Austria are most famous for them, with the best German examples of course being made from Riesling. Canada too makes ice-wine, here spelt in the English way, mostly from a hybrid grape called Vidal, or from Riesling. Canadian ice-wine can be made more reliably than the German equivalent as the winter frosts come sooner and more severely. Freezing grapes concentrates the sugars, like *Botrytis*, but the acidity is concentrated even more efficiently so the best German and Austrian Eisweins have the most amazing freshness on the palate, and because the fruit has not been affected by *Botrytis*, or at least not as much, there is an amazing purity of fruit flavour.

Canadian ice-wine has only been permitted to be exported to the European Union since 2000. Prior to that it fell foul of an EU ruling that forbade the import of sweet light wines from non-EU countries without a special derogation. Technically the import of wines with a total alcohol content – that is the combination of the actual alcohol and the potential alcohol of the residual sugar – over 15 per cent was forbidden. Originally the rule was meant to stop people importing strong wines from outside the then EEC, and using them to boost and stretch EEC wines. The rule was never intended to keep

out good wines, and indeed Hungarian Tokay has always been permitted, so it made sense for the authorities in Brussels to make a derogation in the case. Vidal has lower acidity than Riesling and less pure fruit, but gives a zesty, sherbet-like flavour.

Dried grapes

The production of sweet light wines from dried grapes is almost entirely restricted to Italy, and even these are specialities that are rarely seen on the export markets. Vin Santo, made in various parts of the country but particularly in Tuscany, is perhaps the best known, and can usually be found in Italian delicatessen around Christmas time, even if not at any other time of the year. Vin Santo is the best wine to drink with amaretti biscuits.

Others that you might be able to get occasionally include Reccioto de Soave, a sweet wine made from the same grapes as normal Soave, but dried in barns for a few months before pressing, to encourage evaporation of the water content of the grapes, and Passito de Pantellaria, a Muscat-based sweetie from islands around Sicily.

Whichever of these you get, you will notice a raisin, dried grape, character on the nose. In the case of the Muscat-based wines, this will be dominated by the grape character, in the other cases perhaps more by the subsequent ageing – oxidative for Vin Santo, reductive for Soave.

grapes drying on straw mats for passito wine production

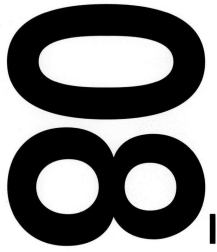

light-bodied red wines

Warm summer days and light meals call for wines that are refreshing and flavoursome, without excessive alcohol and with low tannin. All over the world light red wines are made to satisfy that need – for occasions when such wines as Châteauneuf-du-Pape or red Zinfandel are just too full and tannic, simply too big. Cherry-scented crisp, possibly lightly chilled Beaujolais comes to mind immediately, but it is far from being the only bottle to reach for.

Wines of this sort are often made using a special technique called carbonic maceration or *maceration carbonique*. Here, whole bunches of black grapes are placed in a carbon dioxide atmosphere and the initial stages of fermentation happen because of enzymes within the berry, rather than yeast. After a few days the cell structure of the berries collapses and the grapes are pressed and the juice fermented as for white wine. This results in good levels of colour extracted from the insides of the skins, but because the skins have not been broken through crushing and pumping over, low levels of tannin are extracted.

Other wines are made conventionally, but since colour tends to be released from the skins before, and more easily than tannin, a short maceration will give reasonable colour but lower tannin.

Invariably wines like this lack the structure to age, but this should not be a problem. They are meant to be drunk while they still have their youthful vibrancy. Only if they have been in stock at your wine shop for too long does

their inability to age become a problem. Buy the latest vintage you can, preferably last year's harvest, or the previous one if you must.

Beaujolais

The success of Beaujolais has long been built on the success of 'Nouveau', the first wine of the new vintage, released in November each year with great razzmatazz. At one stage the wine could not be released from the

fresh Beaujolais tastes like an alcoholic version of cherry juice

producers' cellars until just past midnight on November 15 and there were races to get the first bottles to the thirsty Parisian and London restaurants. Changes in the distribution rules mean that it now comes out on the third Thursday in November, and can be released to distribution warehouses before then. These changes make life a lot easier for the retailer and distributor but some of the excitement has inevitably been lost too. Wines shipped in this way will be the lightest of all Beaujolais, and really should be drunk as soon as they are landed. Shops dread having any stock remaining after Christmas as no one will buy it then.

But there is more to Beaujolais than just Nouveau. The area, like so many in France, has a hierarchy of vineyards. As well as Nouveau there is Beaujolais, Beaujolais-Villages and the ten cru areas in the north; areas such as St. Amour, Julienas and Fleurie. There is a distinct family resemblance that runs through them, a result of the grape and climate, but the Villages and cru wines have more character and more structure than the basic.

Trying Beaujolais

To experience the full vibrancy of youth buy a bottle of the Nouveau as soon as it comes out, but get a bottle of inexpensive normal Beaujolais at the same time. This should be the previous vintage, at this level anything earlier will certainly be too tired. Compare the two. Note the vivid blue-red colour of the Nouveau and the aroma of the freshest fruit – cherry and strawberry are common descriptors. You may pick up hints of banana as well, a result of the fermentation technique. The old wine should still be fruity, but lack the vibrancy and nerve of the new wine.

Go on to compare a villages wine with one or more of the crus. In true French style these will never say Beaujolais on the label, so you need to look for one of the names listed at the end of the chapter. The Villages wine will be fuller than the ordinary one, but less complex than the cru, assuming they are from equally good producers. Even the cru wine has a lightness of touch that makes it exceptionally drinkable. Without being weak in either alcohol or flavour, these wines are never blockbusters.

Once you are hooked, you will want to try the various crus. Each has its own character but this will vary from producer to producer, so try to get as many of the 10

summer fruit – strawberry, raspberry and cherry – all are associated with lighter styles of red wine

from the same supplier as possible, and preferably from the same vintage. The differences are subtle, but definitely there. The following list gives the textbook differences so you can compare your results with the 'standard'.

The ten crus of Beaujolais

- **Brouilly** the largest cru, producing full-flavoured wines, perhaps a little more rustic than some crus
- **Côte de Brouilly** more intense than Brouilly, with finer and purer fruit
- **Chenas** generous and full-flavoured wines
- **Chiroubles** one of the lightest of the crus. Very aromatic and reminiscent of strawberries
- **Fleurie** can be quite structured wines for their type, with a fresh fruit and violet nose
- **Juliénas** quite structured and therefore capable of more ageing than many, with a distinct spiciness to the nose
- **Morgon** these wines usually display quite powerful fruit, with a light but firm structure
- **Moulin-à-Vent** perhaps the deepest in colour and firmest on the palate of all the crus
- **Régnié** the newest recruit to the band. Generally ligher than its neighbours, with clean fruit but low tannin
- **St. Amour** it may be just the power of suggestion, but this is always described as the most seductive of the 10 crus. Soft and velvety in texture, and medium bodied compared to the others.

The Loire

After Beaujolais, the Loire is the most renowned region for this style of wine. As we have seen in previous chapters, the Loire produces many excellent whites, but it comes as a surprise to most people outside France to find that only about half of Loire production is white, the rest being divided between red, rosé and sparkling. Most of the reds are drunk locally or in Paris, where they are highly appreciated for their lightness and delicacy, the ideal brasserie wine.

Reds are made in three of the Loire's four sub-regions, although those of the middle areas, Anjou-Saumur and Touraine, are by far the most famous. Look out for appellations such as Saumur Champigny, Chinon, Bourgieul and St Nicolas de Bourgueil, made from Cabernet Franc, and the Touraine appellation, where the grape is usually included on the label – Gamay, Cabernet and Cot (Malbec) are all available. In Sancerre, the red wines are made from Pinot Noir but they maintain their Loire identity – these are not Burgundy lookalikes.

Wherever in the Loire you taste from, there is a family resemblance, perhaps even more so in the reds than the whites. The Cabernet-based wines all have lightness and a fresh, slightly green, stalky fruitiness that is very pleasant in good vintages, but which appear as a green, underripe flavour in other years.

Gamay is easier to ripen, but if Beaujolais is light and fruity, here the style is even more so. Generally very light and fruity, the Touraine Gamay can seem like white wine with added colour. There are exceptions. Good producers in warm vintages can make some serious wines, even some that can age, but these really are exceptions.

Rest of France

Pinot Noir is a grape ideally suited to this type of wine. Not the classic Grand Crus of Burgundy, but certainly the lesser wines of Burgundy, the lowly 'Bourgogne' appellation wines, along with most of the reds of Mâcon, just north of Beaujolais, where Pinot Noir and Gamay can be blended together. Alsace too makes Pinot, generally in a lighter style although this is changing and the wines are gradually getting fuller and richer. As we have seen, Sancerre makes a little red wine, all from Pinot. Full of lively strawberry flavours, this wine can be quite delicious when young.

Italy

Wine is a daily part of the Italian diet, which goes some way to explaining why the majority of Italian wine sold is simple table wine – Vino da Tavola. Most wines are not put on a pedestal here, they are simple, everyday drinks, with the more serious wines, many among the finest in the world, being reserved for special occasions. As a result, most Italian red wine is light, fruity and easy to drink.

This is also true of many of the more basic levels of some DOC and even DOCG wines (the higher categories in wine law). We will look at Chianti in the medium-bodied section, but much of the cheaper wine – the sort that once would have appeared in the basket-covered *fiasci* – is far lighter. For the majority of the lighter styles, look to the north of the country. Wines such as Valpolicella and Bardolino from Veneto and Merlot from Friuli are perfect examples.

Valpolicella, made from the local Cornvina and Mondelara, comes in a range of styles. For this exercise, buy the simplest form (avoid the classico designation and keep well away from the Amarone and Reciotto versions for this tasting. These are delicious rarities but they are at the opposite end of the wine spectrum). Taste this and compare it to the Beaujolais. You should find the character is different, with more of the cherry characters, sharper, crisper fruit, and this is backed up on the palate by a refreshing acidic tang, and a more savoury flavour.

Bardolino is Valpolicella's neighbour in Veneto, made from the same local grapes. It takes the light, fruity character to an extreme, and is perfect wine for a summer picnic. Again, the classico area produces fuller wines, but even these are light and fruity. Try also the varietal wines of northern Italy, in particular Merlot and Pinot Nero (Pinot Noir). These will be, perhaps, more familiar flavours, and again in the light fruity mould.

Also light bodied, but in a different style all together, is Lambrusco, mostly seen in its medium-sweet screw-capped table wine version. Try to find a DOC Lambrusco, as young as possible, to taste the true wine. The table wine version has done a great deal of good as it has encouraged novice wine drinkers, but at the same time it has all but destroyed the market for the 'proper' wine. The DOC wines will be sealed with a proper cork, not a screw cap, and generally are drier, although usually not totally dry. If fresh, these are delicious, and, given that they come from near Bologna, the ideal accompaniment for that old stand-by, spaghetti Bolognaise – the crisp acid and the light effervescence balancing the strong tomato flavours and cutting through the oil.

Germany

German red wines are rarely seen on the export markets, being far more highly prized within the country than elsewhere. Most are in the lighter styles, with a handful of producers managing to make medium-bodied wines from Spätburgunder, the German name for Pinot Noir, but most are far lighter. Dornfelder is Germany's second most important grape, giving deep colours but very light fruity styles of wine.

Iberia

Most of the reds from Spain and Portugal are too full to be included in this chapter, being at least medium-bodied, but there are a handful of exceptions. Think of Spanish reds and you probably think of the full, oaky flavours of a Rioja Reserva, but many Spanish regions, including Rioja, produce wines for immediate drinking, or Vinos Jovens. Generally light to medium bodied, these will not have seen any oak maturation and are not designed for bottle maturation either.

In Portugal the range of light-bodied wines is even more restricted, even the simplest of Portugal's DOCs generally makes something a little too full for this section. There is one very notable exception, a complete oddity from the north of the country – red Vinho Verde. This light alcohol – typically only 9 or 10 per cent – wine has massively deep colour with screechingly high acidity and rasping tannin, yet has a light body, and oddly light fruit too. This is not a wine you will find on every shelf in the export markets. If you want to try it, and I recommend you try everything once, you will have to find a specialist Portuguese delicatessen, or visit the country itself.

Red Vinho Verde has a classic style, albeit in a very odd way. It will never appeal to a wide, international audience. One other light wine made in Portugal is designed to do just that. Sogrape, the biggest wine producer in Portugal, have developed Dão Nova, which is made in the same way as Beaujolais.

New World

The high quality wines of the New World tend to be too full bodied to be included here, being at least medium bodied, but the lesser wines of all the major brands are lighter. Basic level Gallo, Jacob's Creek and their contemporaries are just as light as anything else we are looking at here.

One notable New World wine that we should consider here is the Australian Tarrango, a grape developed to give naturally high acids, low tannins and a light body. This, with the juicy fruit flavours, makes for a very refreshing glass of wine.

6 medium and medium-to-full-bodied reds

The majority of famous red wines are medium bodied, rather than light or really full. Like medium-sweet whites, there is a vast range of styles, and many of the wines we will look at here can fall into the full-bodied section in good vintages, or when young. Others would have been considered full in the past, before the modern heavyweight wines of Australia and California, and increasingly Chile or South Africa, came onto the market. This chapter is, therefore, longer than the others on red wines.

Because of both style and the vast range available, medium-bodied reds are the most versatile of red wines, complementing the greatest range of foods. All the classic food wines of France, Italy and Spain fall into this category, as of course do the New World wines made from the same grapes, provided they are grown in less hot areas. Some grapes nearly always give medium weight in the finished wine – Pinot Noir, Tempranillo and Sangiovese are classics. They can be made in other styles, but these are the exceptions. Others, such as Cabernet Sauvignon and Merlot, give medium-bodied wines in their natural homes, but fuller weight when grown in the hotter climates of Australia and California. With other varieties is it the viticulture rather than the climate that alters the style. Low-yielding vineyards in the Cape can give some very full-bodied Pinotage, but the majority is higher yielding, giving medium weight.

Given the size of the subject, we will look at the wines in this chapter by region in Europe, and then by grape variety.

France

Bordeaux and Burgundy are the two classic red wine regions of France. Equally famous, and at their best equally expensive, it is far too easy to talk about them in the same breath, as if they are more similar than different. To start this section we will look at the distinctions between the two regions, and the differences in the resulting styles. We will then go on to look at the differences between styles within the two regions.

Bordeaux and Burgundy have far more differences than similarities. Bordeaux is a large region – the largest of all French AC regions – on the Atlantic coast in south-western France. The climate here is dominated by the Atlantic, and by the Gironde, the estuary of the Dordogne and the Garonne. Burgundy is inland, further north and well away from any maritime influence, so it enjoys a continental climate, one of greater extremes. As a result, the grapes grown are completely different, with an obvious effect on the wine styles.

Classic red Burgundy is made from Pinot Noir. The only other black grape allowed is Gamay, and that only in the south of Burgundy for Beaujolais and Mâcon. Pinot Noir is now grown in many other parts of the world too, but this north-east quadrant of France is its natural home. With very rare exceptions, Burgundy is unblended.

By contrast, red Bordeaux, also known by its traditional English name, Claret, is almost invariably a blend of three varieties. Merlot is the most widely planted grape in the region, with Cabernet Sauvignon and Cabernet Franc dominating in some districts within the region. Merlot generally gives softer wines with higher alcohol and soft, plummy fruit, whereas the Cabernets are more structured, with firmer tannins, perhaps not such high alcohol and a smell of blackcurrant when young, which develops into all manner of different aromas with age. Cabernet Franc is a related variety that we have already looked at in an unblended form from the Loire. Most Bordeaux châteaux will grow all three grapes, partly as a sort of insurance policy and also in order to add complexity to the blend. The insurance policy is because near the coast the weather patterns are unpredictable so in some years the Cabernet will ripen best, in others the Merlot.

Burgundy is also far smaller, particularly if you consider only the central Côte d'Or, the heart of Burgundy – typically producing about a quarter as much wine as Bordeaux. This, along with one of the most complex appellation hierarchies with hundreds of individual wine names, makes Burgundy a fascinating area, but one often described as a minefield for the consumer.

Both areas' AC structure divides the wines, in ascending order of individuality, into regional (AC Bordeaux, AC Bourgogne), district (e.g. Médoc or Mâcon) and commune, or individual parish AC (e.g. Pauillac or Gervey-Chambertin). In Bordeaux the higher classifications are outside the AC system, so for example Château Latour, a Premier cru classé in the 1855 classification, is Appellation Pauillac, a commune appellation. The highest rated vineyards in Burgundy each has its own appellation, often for minute plots of land. Le Chambertin and La Tâche are individual ACs in their own right, each smaller than many Bordeaux châteaux.

Taste the difference

To see the difference between Bordeaux and Burgundy, buy a bottle of commune-level wine from each area. This is an ideal exercise for a dinner party. Ideally, start with a Burgundy from the Côte de Nuit, the northern section of the Côte d'Or. Nuits St Georges and Gevrey-Chambertin are probably the easiest to come across. Pair this with one of the famous Médoc communes – Margaux, St Julien, Pauillac or St Estèphe. Try to get wines of a similar age, but preferably not venerable examples – great age tends to dilute the initial differences between wines.

The wines will be very different in colour. Pinot Noir is a grape that gives great flavour, and has the ability to give enormous complexity – perhaps more than any other black grape, but it rarely gives deep-coloured wines. Médoc wines, by contrast, are based on Cabernet Sauvignon. This grape has small berries and therefore a greater skin to pulp ratio, leading to deeper colours and greater tannin. Not only is the depth of colour different, the actual hue is different. Pinot Noir tends to turn browner at a younger age than Cabernet Sauvignon, so the Burgundy will appear older than the claret.

The noses will be very different. Pinot Noir when young smells of raspberries and strawberries – real summer pudding aroma – with a perfumed top nose of violets. As it matures the nose changes towards a more vegetal character, reminiscent of cabbage or cauliflower, and with further ageing this develops into something that is politely referred to as 'farmyardy'. If all this sound horribly derogatory about the grape, rest assured, it isn't. These really are terms of affection when it comes to Pinot Noir.

Young Cabernet, by contrast, smells of blackcurrants. If you have bought a reasonable quality wine this may well

Merlot is often described as tasting plummy

raspberries are associated with young Pinot Noir

be overlaid in youth with a hint of vanilla, or of cinnamon from the wood maturation. In cool areas, and especially in cold vintages, you may well get hints of green capsicum (bell pepper) too. More mature examples might be more herbal, more savoury perhaps on the nose, with hints of tobacco, cigar boxes or even meat.

There is no way of telling how much Cabernet Sauvignon or Merlot is in the blend for Bordeaux, unless you speak to the wine maker. Some reference books give figures but usually they are out of date by the time they are published, and only give the percentages in the vineyard, which may or may not correspond with the contents of the blend. It is possible, therefore, that your Médoc wine will be higher on the plummy, fleshier Merlot.

When you taste the two, notice how the structure on the palate is completely different. Both are dry, and medium in alcohol, although the Burgundy may be a little higher. Both will be medium to full bodied, neither is likely to be either light or very full. But they are different. Pinot Noir relies on acidity for preservation rather than tannin, which tends to be low in this grape except in very special vintages. What you should find, therefore, is a wine with crisp acidity, warming alcohol and a mouth-filling flavour that has an elegance about it, hopefully with an almost ethereal flavour on the aftertaste.

The Médoc is capable of just as much elegance, and you will be hoping for complexity here too, but the structure of the wine is totally different. Firm tannins hold everything together alongside medium rather than high acidity. The Merlot in the blend comes through as a richness and softness in the middle palate, filling the frame that is the Cabernet's structure.

Getting to know Bordeaux

The best place to start when trying to understand the styles of the great Bordeaux reds is the great divide between left and right banks. On the Gironde is a vast body of water, with a huge influence on the climate of the area. It divides the area in two, with the Graves district, the Haut Médoc and Médoc on one side of the Garonne and then the Gironde and St Emilion, Pomerol, Bourg and Blaye on the far side of the Dordogne and Gironde. Wines of the Médoc are often called left-bank wines, those of St Emilion and Pomerol are referred to as right bank. The big difference is the grapes mix. The gravel soil of Graves and Médoc favour the Cabernets, whereas the more mixed soils on the other side favour Merlot. To compare the two taste a St Emilion alongside a Médoc. Be careful to buy wines of a similar age, at similar prices. Notice how the St Emilion seems softer, more generous and warming, with less tannin and higher alcohol. This is the Merlot dominating the blend.

Within Bordeaux and the Médoc in particular, there is clearly defined hierarchy of appellations and also a clear classification of châteaux. Often the two don't sit well together, so there are wines, in theory, of lower appellations that are consistently better than those from one of the higher reputed areas. To see how the appellation system works, when it works, do a comparative tasting of a basic AC Bordeaux, an Haut-Médoc and a basic wine from one of the four great communes within the area – Margaux, St Julien, Pauillac or St Estèphe. For this exercise, avoid wines that name themselves after the château and choose wines from one of the big merchant houses instead.

The Bordeaux AC wine can come from anywhere in the region, and will probably be based on Merlot. The yields will be relatively high, and if the wine has been made to reach a particular price point, it will, hopefully, be correct, and easy drinking, but that will be about all.

The Haut-Médoc will have stricter rules as to provenance – coming only from the left bank of the Gironde. The rules governing its production will be stricter too, with lower yields being the most obvious difference. This will give greater depth of flavour, more Cabernet influence because of the soil here, and probably more use of wood, because the producer can afford that sort of luxury on these more expensive wines. Note that all the vines in the Médoc could be used to make basic Bordeaux, if the producer chose to work to the more relaxed rules.

The single commune wine will be more concentrated, and you should find more of the influence of the commune. Each has its own slightly different character. Margaux is softest and has often been described as more feminine than the others. St Julien has a finesse about it, without being too delicate, Pauillac is the most powerful of the four, and St Estèphe can be the most austere in youth.

The Médoc has a multi-layered hierarchy of châteaux as well as appellations. At the top are the cru classés, subdivided into five levels. This classification is historic, based on the prices fetched for the wines in the years before the list was drawn up in 1855. With just one significant change – the promotion of Château Mouton Rothschild in 1973 – and a handful of changes of name, the current list is unchanged from the original.

The top end wines, and particularly the Premier and Deuxième cru classés, have become luxury goods, or blue-chip investments rather than wines that most can afford.

Far more affordable, and sometimes of the same quality, are the cru bourgeois. Some of these are now becoming as expensive as cru classé wines, but the majority are very fine, at prices that, while not being everyday drinking, are at least within reach.

Still better value are the cru artisan, wines with real character in good vintages, but without the cachet of the others. Below these are the hundreds of producers without any specific classification.

Other wines from Cabernet and Merlot

The world is as much in love with Cabernet Sauvignon and Merlot as it is with Chardonnay. There is hardly a wine-producing country on earth that does not grow these two, used either singly or in blends with each other or with other varieties. From France these grapes have travelled to other Western European countries, to Eastern Europe, South Africa, the Americas and Australasia.

Bulgaria made its name on the export markets with Cabernet. Cabernet Sauvignon, at the price of the cheapest Vin de Table, yet equal in quality and similar in style to mid-priced Bordeaux, flew out of the doors of off-licences and supermarkets in the 1980s and early 1990s. In the UK at least, Bulgaria is the unsung hero of varietal labelling; it was Bulgaria that first introduced the great British public to the concept of Cabernet Sauvignon, and by extension, to varietal labelling as a whole. Try a Bulgarian Cabernet in contrast to a Bordeaux of a similar price – not long ago you would have been guaranteed a better wine for your money from Bulgaria, but at the time of writing, Bulgaria is going through a problem patch, and this is not the case.

In the New World, Cabernet has become one of the great standards, with Merlot becoming more popular each year. As with Bordeaux, they are often judiciously blended, even if it does not say so on the label. For example, Californian Cabernets may be up to 25 per cent something else, whereas for Australian and South African versions the minimum Cabernet content is 85 per cent.

The closest of these to the French style is South Africa, where the crisp acidity and relatively restrained fruit make the wines a bridge between Old and New World styles. Australia and California usually go for the full, up-front fruity style, medium or full bodied depending on the market segment they are aiming at – the fuller the better.

California initially went down the pure varietal route, but increasingly the standard 'Bordeaux blend' of Cabernet Sauvignon and Merlot, even with some Cabernet Franc, is being used.

The latest fashion in Californian wine is pure Merlot. This stems from the realization that red wine has certain health-giving properties, and that Merlot, grown in these warm vineyards, gives a rich, supple wine with warming alcohol, often 14 per cent or so, without the hard tannins of Cabernet. Compare both Cabernets and Merlots labelled simply as Californian with those from more specific regions. Napa and Sonoma are particularly high quality, but St Ynes, Alexander Valley and Mendocino are worth looking out for.

1855 Classification of the Médoc (communes in brackets)

First growths (premiers crus)

Château Haut-Brion Pessac (Graves)
Château Lafite-Rothschild (Pauillac)
Château Latour (Pauillac)
Château Margaux (Margaux)
Château Mouton-Rothschild (Pauillac)

Second growths (deuxièmes crus)

Château Brane-Cantenac Cantenac (Margaux)
Château Cos d'Estournel (Saint-Estèphe)
Château Ducru-Beaucaillou (Saint-Julien)
Château Durfort-Vivens (Margaux)
Château Gruaud-Larose (Saint-Julien)
Château Lascombes (Margaux)
Château Léoville-Barton (Saint-Julien)
Château Léoville-Les Cases (Saint-Julien)
Château Léoville-Poyferré (Saint-Julien)
Château Montrose (Saint-Estèphe)
Château Pichon-Longueville-Baron (Pauillac)
Château Pichon-Longueville, Comtesse de Lalande (Pauillac)
Château Rausan-Gassies (Margaux)
Château Rausan-Ségla (Margaux)

Third growths (troisièmes crus)

Château Boyd-Cantenac Cantenac (Margaux)
Château Calon-Ségur (Saint-Estèphe)
Château Cantenac-Brown Cantenac (Margaux)
Château Desmirail (Margaux)
Château d'Issan Cantenac (Margaux)
Château Ferrière (Margaux)
Château Giscours Labarde (Margaux)
Château Kirwan Cantenac (Margaux)
Château Lagrange (Saint-Julien)
Château La Lagune Ludon (Haut-Médoc)
Château Langoa-Barton (Saint-Julien)
Château Malescot Saint-Exupéry (Margaux)
Château Marquis d'Alesme-Becker (Margaux)
Château Palmer Cantenac (Margaux)

Fourth growths (quatrièmes crus)

Château Beychevelle (Saint-Julien)
Château Branaire-Ducru (Saint-Julien)
Château Duhart-Milon-Rothschild (Pauillac)
Château Lafon-Rochet (Saint-Estèphe)
Château La Tour-Carnet Saint-Laurent (Haut Médoc)
Château Marquis-de-Terme (Margaux)
Château Pouget Cantenac (Margaux)
Château Prieuré-Lichine Cantenac (Margaux)
Château Saint-Pierre (Saint-Julien)
Château Talbot (Saint-Julien)

Fifth growths (cinquièmes crus)

Château Batailley (Pauillac)
Château Belgrave Saint-Laurent (Haut-Médoc)
Château Cantemerle Macau (Haut-Médoc)
Château Clerc-Milon (Pauillac)
Château Cos-Labory (Saint-Estèphe)
Château Croizet-Bages (Pauillac)
Château D'Armailhac (Pauillac)
Château Dauzac Labarde (Margaux)
Château de Camensac Saint-Laurent (Haut-Médoc)
Château du Tertre Arsac (Margaux)
Château Grand-Puy-Ducasse (Pauillac)
Château Grand-Puy-Lacoste (Pauillac)
Château Haut-Bages-Libéral (Pauillac)
Château Haut-Batailley (Pauillac)
Château Lynch-Bages (Pauillac)
Château Lynch-Moussas (Pauillac)
Château Pédesclaux (Pauillac)
Château Pontet-Canet (Pauillac)

(Acknowledgements CIVB, Bordeaux)

In Australia the main blending component for Cabernet is Shiraz. This combination, never legally seen on a French appellation wine, is widely used at all quality levels. Both varieties will be stated on the label, with the first being the predominant. Compare Cabernet-Shiraz with a Shiraz Cabernet at about the same price level to see how each variety behaves in the blend. You could even include a pure Cabernet and a pure Shiraz for good measure.

As in California, blending between areas in Australia is commonplace, either to provide sufficient raw material for a big brand – note that the Australian wine industry has set itself the target of becoming the world's biggest supplier of branded wine – or in order to make the highest quality wines possible. This goes against everything the French AC system stands for, along with the Italian DOC, Spanish DO, etc. but the logic is clear. Why should a wine be better just because it comes from a small region?

Some of the best wines in the world are blends of component parts from different districts within a region – Champagne and Port are classic examples – and the Australians take this further, tracking grapes over vast distances. As a result, and despite all the publicity about regionality that gets published in the consumer wine press, the 'appellation' is of less importance than the brand. All the big makers, companies such as Penfold's and Hardy's, produce a clear hierarchy of brands aimed at different sectors of the market. The cheaper wines will all be labelled 'South Eastern Australia' at least in the EU. This vast area that takes in three states and the majority of the wine produced in the country, is in response to a European rule that forbids the sale in the EU of wines that state the grape variety without a region.

To see how the wine industry works, try wines from the same producer at different price/quality levels. If you use Hardy's look for Banrock Station, Stamp Collection and the specific vineyards. For Penfold's, look for the different bin numbers at different price points. You will find a greater concentration of fruit as you go up. This is largely due to the fruit sourcing. The cheaper wines will be based on the big, irrigated vineyard areas such as Riverina and Riverland, whereas the finer wines will have a greater input from the finer areas for example, Barossa, Coonawarra or Yarra.

Many of the finest wines are from single estates, and of course these will state the region on the label. For a detailed experience of Australia, get hold of Cabernets of about the same price point from different areas. The differences are more muted here than in Bordeaux, and they can be overridden by the wine-making influence, but you will probably find the Barossa version fuller and richer than that from Coonawarra. Yarra Valley and Western Australia tend to produce less up-front wines with slightly crisper acidity.

Getting to know Burgundy

The appellation system in in Burgundy is more complex than in Bordeaux. Here there are five levels, with both Premier Cru and Grand Cru being separate AC categories. To make matters worse, the vineyards are often owned by dozens of individuals. Selection of a good producer is more important here than the choice of AC.

To get to know the region well would take a lifetime, such is the variety available, but as a starting point, look at the different quality levels. Compare a basic Bourgogne Rouge (regional AC) with a wine from a single commune – Nuits St Georges and Gevrey-Chambertin are widely available. To take this further, taste a Premier Cru and/or a Grand Cru level wine. Be warned, Grand Cru Burgundies are made in small quantities and enjoy massive demand, they should never be cheap. Notice how both the intensity and complexity grow as you move up the scale, but even the fullest will always be lighter, and less structured and tannic than a Bordeaux of a similar price.

Other Pinots

Pinot Noir has long been seen as the Holy Grail for wine makers elsewhere. For a long time it was perceived as a difficult grape, but now the right sites have been found, there are stunning wines being made all over the world. If you like good Pinot, search out the cooler climate versions, such as Oregon and Washington State in the USA, or the Carneros region of California, where the sea fogs keep the vines cool.

Some of Australia's best Pinots come from Yarra and from Tasmania, where again the climate is cooler. Perhaps the greatest success for Pinot has been in New Zealand, where it is now the most widely planted black variety. The area that has specialized particularly in this grape in Marlborough, on the southerly tip of the North Island.

The Rhône and the south of France

The wines of the Rhône are generally considered full bodied, but if we are honest, most are medium bodied. True, the finest Cornas or Hermitage, Châteauneuf-du-Pape or Côte Rôtie will be as full bodied as can be, but the majority of Côtes du Rhône, Côtes du Rhône Villages and even wines such as Gigondas and Vacqueyras tend to be medium, or medium to full. Many of the more basic Côtes du Rhônes are really quite light.

The wines of southern France mostly fall into this category too. Wines such as Bandol can be very full, but Minervois, Fitou and the red Vin de Pays are mostly medium bodied. Compare these to the wines of the Rhône. There is a distinct family resemblance, both having a Mediterranean climate that favours a certain selection of grape varieties. The wines here are usually blends of varieties, often with Grénache as the main component.

Classic reds from Iberia

Grenache, or Garnacha, is the main black grape of Spain too, where it is often blended with Spain's more famous grape, Tempranillo. These two make up the blend in Rioja; in Navarra, where they are often joined by international varieties; in Ribera del Duero and in many other parts of the country. Where blends are not used, much of the wine is from Tempranillo.

Taste a range of these wines. Often, though by no means exclusively, there will be liberal use of American oak in the maturation, giving very noticeable spice and coconut flavours.

In the middle of the country the vast, arid plain of La Mancha makes reasonable red wines from Cencibel, the local name for Tempranillo. Never great, these are of increasingly sound quality. A far better area, just to the south of La Mancha, is Valdepeñas, which is still firmly in the inexpensive category.

Across the border in Portugal the mix of grapes used becomes far broader, with scores of wines being a blend of many varieties. The classic DOC areas of Dão Bairrada and the Douro are today joined by up and coming areas in the Ribatejo and the Alentejo. Most wines are made from local varieties. International favourites are grown in Portugal, but to a very limited extent as most wine makers there are great believers in the intrinsic qualities of their local varieties.

Italy's medium-bodied wines

Chianti is one of the most famous wines ever made. Coming from Tuscany, made mainly from Sangiovese, this is one wine that even non-wine drinkers have heard of. It has developed over the years to accompany the local food so has a classic combination of elevated acidity to cut through the olive oil and medium to firm tannins.

The best Chiantis come from the classico area, the picturesque hillsides between Florence and Siena. Wines labelled Chianti, without the classico designation, come from a wide area surrounding the original heartland of the region. Compare a basic Chianti with a classico and ideally add in a riserva version, which will have spent more time ageing in wood before sale. Don't expect to get lots of oak flavours though, the Italians tend to favour large old wood vats rather than small barrels.

Related to Chianti are the other two Sangiovese wines of Tuscany, Brunello di Montalcino and Vino Nobile di Montepulciano. Compare the three. Typically Vino Nobile di Montepulciano is very similar to Chianti, if perhaps a little weightier, whereas Brunello is far more robust, with great concentration of fruit. A less robust, younger and therefore cheaper version is Rosso di Montalcino, made from the same grapes, but blended from the less intense vats.

Don't confuse Vino Nobile di Montepulciano with the grape variety Montepulciano, which makes light- to medium-bodied red wine in the east of the country, particularly in Abruzzo.

Italy is usually considered to be the largest wine-producing nation so it is not surprising that the range of wines is so immense. In many cases these are meant to accompany local food, which is a theme that would work for the whole of this chapter. Medium and medium-to-full-bodied reds are extremely versatile drinks, with an enormous range of styles to keep most wine drinkers happy.

# full-bodied red wines

After a long walk on a cold winter's evening, there is nothing more comforting than a hearty casserole and a glass of something full, rich and flavoursome. Full-bodied reds are the ideal accompaniment to full-flavoured food, from a simple stew or barbecued steak to a fine game dish. For the vegetarian, the intensity of aubergine (egg plant) and tomato in ratatouille demands a Mediterranean style of wine to match.

How full is full?

The accepted definition of 'full-bodied' is changing as an increasing number of wines are getting fuller and more alcoholic. Wines that once were seen as very full, and quoted as examples of the fullest wines you could get, such as the southern Rhône Châteauneuf-du-Pape, and even the Piemontese Barolo, are not as full as many newer wines such as top Australian Shiraz, or premium, single estate Californian Zinfandel. The greater weight of the New World offerings results from greater ripeness in their grapes. By contrast, as we will see, many wines traditionally sold as full bodied are nothing of the sort, in particular the less expensive Côtes du Rhône wines made for immediate consumption.

In Chapter 9 there were many wines that could be called full bodied in some circumstances and medium in others. In this chapter we will concentrate on really full-bodied wines.

Body is often seen as a function of alcohol, but pure ethanol is less dense than water, so this is only part of the story. It is possible to find high-alcohol wines that are not particularly full in the mouth, but some wines at around 12 per cent, these days considered medium alcohol, can be quite full. Both alcohol and body result from ripeness of fruit, so most full-bodied reds come from warm climates, or from hot vintages in cooler areas. Some grape varieties tend to give fuller wines than others too, so Syrah, whether from its original home of the northern Rhône or as Shiraz in its adopted home in Australia, will tend to be full and weighty, unless it is over-cropped or from a wet year. Mourvèdre, Nebiolo and Touriga Nacional are other classically 'full' varieties. Some grapes will give full wines in some places and medium-bodied ones in others. Cabernet from Coonawarra, for example, is far bigger and richer than even the ripest Médoc, and Tempranillo, Spain's finest black grape, is typically fuller from Priorato and Ribera del Duero than is Rioja.

Yields and wine making play their part too. As we have seen elsewhere, there is a close relationship, all else being equal, between the yield in the vineyard and the fruit intensity in the finished wine. This is also true for the structure and body of the wine. Compare a mass-market Côtes de Rhône with a single estate Côtes de Rhône Villages. You will find a marked increase in concentration in all aspects – colour, flavour and body. The grape mix will be similar, a base of Grénache with a number of other improving varieties like Syrah and Mourvèdre, the climate will have been the same, and if you choose the same vintage, even the weather conditions during the growing season will have been very similar, but the Villages wine will have a lower yield. This lower yield, required by AC law, goes some way to explain why so few Côtes de Rhône Villages wines are seen – many more could be made, but a lot of producers prefer to make larger volumes of the cheaper wine because the extra price that the Villages wine fetches does not compensate for the smaller volumes.

Same shape, different tastes

Shiraz and Syrah

The body of any wine is only one aspect of its character, and there are innumerable different flavours to be had in this, as any other, category. Compare a northern Rhône red such as Hermitage, Côte Rôtie, St Joseph or Cornas to an Australian Shiraz. Spend about the same on each and choose good examples of both. Do not try this with the mass-market versions of either – 'full bodied' on the back label of a big-brand wine is a good sales technique but in fact most are medium to full at best. Spend twice as much and you should get a much fuller wine. Both wines are made from the same grape, and are made in a similar way, although the Australian version is more likely to have seen new oak maturation, yet they smell and taste very different. The Rhône will have the classic pepper character overlaying the dark, brooding fruit. Tannins will be quite high but may well be somewhat masked by the richness of the fruit. The Australian version will seem softer, with lower acidity, and will perhaps seem fuller depending on the wine you choose, but most important it tastes different. Yes, there is a family resemblance, but the pepper character of the Rhône will not be there, whatever your wine merchant has told you, replaced by greater concentration of sweet, dark berry fruit and most likely noticeable smoky, vanilla oak and possibly a sweeter spiciness, cinnamon or all-spice flavours.

Cabernet and Merlot

As we have seen in some detail, Cabernet Sauvignon gives medium-bodied, or sometimes even light-bodied, wines in its natural home but it has travelled the world and there can now be few countries where wine is made that do not have some Cabernet vineyards. Hotter climes can result in some very full versions. Try an Australian Cabernet, preferably from a named estate and from the region of Coonawarra, and an American version. Here the Napa Valley is considered the finest, but equally full examples can come from Sonoma, St Ynes Valley and Alexander Valley. Think back to the Bordeaux examples when you do this – there are considerable differences in both weight and flavour.

Merlot too can give a more full-bodied wine than you are ever likely to get from St Emilion. One country that has made a particular success with its Merlot wines is the USA – notably the Pacific Northwest and California – where, once the fashion started to change drinking from whites to reds, Merlot became flavour of the month. Try a premium Californian example against the Cabernet. Leave the basic versions on the shelf for now, we are looking at full-bodied wines and only the premium estates make Merlot in a truly full-bodied style. Note that the same differences we found in the St Emilion and Médoc comparison are still there in the warmer fruit, but that the nose is far more fruit dominant, the alcohol higher and the tannins less noticeable.

In other countries too, the Bordeaux pair, Merlot and Cabernet, is capable of making some full wines, although the standard examples from South Africa and Chile, New Zealand or Uruguay tend to be more medium to full. The exceptions, as so often, are the premium wines.

Other grapes

Italy makes some very full-bodied reds, nearly all from local varieties, many of which are rarely seen outside Italy, and even if they are, they seldom get the same cachet as Cabernet or Chardonnay. These reds most famously come from the north of the country, most notably Piemonte and Veneto, but increasingly we are seeing high quality reds from the southern half of Italy too, with wines such as Aglianico del Vulture from Basilicata and Taurasi from Campania. For an interesting Piemonte tasting get hold of a good quality Barbera d'Alba or Barbera d'Asti and try it alongside our benchmark Barolo. In both cases, the flavours are going to be very different from the Syrah/Shiraz comparison, far more aged without the obvious fruit flavours, more savoury and almost meaty – beef stock or game – in the case of the Barolo. Both wines are full but the acid and tannic structures are very different – Barolo is high in everything whereas the Barbera has high, but not as high, tannin and lower acidity.

Another classic Italian full-bodied wine is Brunello de Montalcino. Brunello is a clone, a sub-variety, of Sangiovese, and here in the heart of Tuscany, Sangiovese is King. Brunello has a very different profile from Chianti though. It tends to be deeper in colour and the fruit is far more rich and concentrated, with less obvious acidity on the palate.

The fullest wines from Veneto are completely different. In Valpolicella most growers make a certain, usually tiny, amount of Amarone. Here parts of the best bunches of the most healthy grapes are removed and set aside to partially dry over the autumn. These concentrated grapes are then crushed and fermented, the concentration of the sugar from drying giving far greater alcohol and flavour intensity, contrasting dramatically with the normal, and even classico, versions we tasted in the lighter-red sections.

Valpolicella, at all levels, is a wine where the dominant character is the fruit. In the Reccioto and Amarone versions, this may well be dried fruit, that is after all how they are made, but it is still the fruit that matters. The southern Italian wines have a different character altogether. Taste an Aglianico del Vulture or a Taurasi and your first impression is going to be one of heat. These are hot vineyards and the wines reflect that with aromas of spice and herbs, perhaps not dissimilar to the flavours found in the biggest wines of the southern Rhône.

Zinfandel, often, if erroneously, called California's native grape, makes vast quantities of very light, pale pink wine sold as blush or White Zinfandel. But the same grape is capable of producing some of the most full-bodied and powerful wines. Taste the premium wines from the region. Notice the dark berry fruits, along with smoke or cedar depending on oak use. Sometimes you will find hints of dark cherry, tar or black pepper. You will often find some dried fruit character, or hot, cooked fruit, from the ripest grapes in the vat.

Like Zinfandel, Pinotage can be made in lighter styles, albeit red rather than blush. To get the full Pinotage effect, though, you need to try one from an unirrigated estate. Pinotage is a grape developed in South Africa by crossing the Burgundian Pinot Noir with the south of France's Cinsault. The result is almost exclusively grown on the Cape, with a minute amount planted in New Zealand. High quality Pinotage is deeply coloured, with a pungent aroma of dark fruit, spice and a slightly strange smell of banana skins – the smell you get when bananas are being unpacked and displayed in a shop.

Portugal's top black grape, Touriga Nacional, is a native of the northern part of the country, both the Douro Valley, home of Port, and the Dão regions. The Douro is most famous for Port, which we will look at in Chapter 12, but it is getting progressively more famous for its light wines too. These were once seen very much as the poor relation, a way of using up the grapes that did not get into the Port blends. Today many Port producers, led by Ramos Pinto, but now joined by many of the other leading names including Niepoort, Sogrape and the Symington group, and a number of individual quintas such as Crasto, are devoting some of their best grapes to light wine. Many of these are based on Touriga Nacional, often blended with other local grapes.

The Dão is a little further south, but also inland and therefore, like the Douro, has a dry climate. In the past the wines here tended to be over-extracted, giving huge tannin which needed long maturation to soften it. This was all too often done in ill-maintained old wood, which dried out the fruit long before the tannins were tamed. Today investment in the region by big firms such as Sogrape, and by an increasing number of individual producers, has led to a sea change in the wines' style. Again, blends are the order of the day, but some varietal wines are now emerging, some from Touriga, others from Jaen and Alfocheiro Preto.

Spain's Tempranillo has always been the backbone of her top red wines. This has always dominated the finest Rioja Reservas and Gran Reservas, but by today's standards these are generally medium full, rather than really full bodied, which is why we looked at them in the previous chapter. The fullest wines from Spain today come from regions further west, the increasingly famous Ribera del Duero (the River Duero is the same river as the Portuguese Douro) and Toro.

Try one of these from a recent vintage and notice the sheer depth of colour, flavour and structure that is now being exported. Whereas Rioja is generally aged for us by the producers, and released when the producers think they are ready, these wines are made in a more modern style. Like New World wines the massive fruit makes them instantly appealing, but the best are capable of long development – cellaring is optional.

sparkling wines

Sparkling wine is the wine of celebration, consumed at parties and receptions, but too often removed from the general wine repertoire as a result. But it is wine, and as such deserves the same consideration as its non-effervescent brethren; perhaps more so given the time and effort that goes into its production, and the cost that we all have to bear when buying it.

Two main factors affect the taste, the raw material – like light wine this encompasses the grapes and their origin – and the way in which the wine has been made sparkling. Most sparkling wine starts life as still wine, but the manufacturing process that gives us the bubbles may also add extra flavours and complexity. Let's look first at how wine is made sparkling, and consider the effect this has.

No one really knows how the first sparkling wine came about but it seems probable that, like so much in life, it was initially a mistake. Perhaps fermentation was prematurely halted by the cold of winter and that wine was then shipped, coming alive again when warmed up in the tavern, or the following spring (wine that had not finished fermenting would have had a viable yeast population just waiting to get back to work on any remaining sugar when the time was right). Maybe sugar was added by the customer and active yeast got to work on that. We will never know, but almost certainly the monk most often quoted as being the inventor of Champagne, Dom Perignon, did no such thing, although he undoubtedly improved the product and it was his research, his care and his attention to detail that first put Champagne on the map as a sparkling wine producer.

Today sparkling wine is made all over the world, and by a number of different methods. The name 'Champagne' has been used indiscriminately in the past as a generic name for all bubbly, both by manufactures and consumers, but it is a protected name for the Appellation Contrôlée wine of the Champagne region in northern France. In this chapter we will use the word Champagne only when referring to the AC product.

How do the bubbles get there?

As must ferments and becomes wine, the yeast enzymes act on sugar to produce alcohol and carbon dioxide. When still wine is being made, this escapes into the atmosphere but for sparkling wine, a certain amount is retained. Usually this is achieved by inducing a secondary fermentation in the still wine, either in tanks or in bottles, but wine can be made to sparkle simply by adding carbon dioxide in the same way as is done to make fizzy drinks. This latter method tends to be used only for very cheap wine, made sparkling cheaply, and although there is nothing intrinsically wrong with the process, most such wines are unexciting to say the least. These are rarely seen in the UK because of our exorbitant tax regime, but are widely available in other countries. The labels of such wines will always state that they are made by injecting carbon dioxide, and so are easy to spot.

All the other wines get their sparkle from a secondary fermentation. This adds both the gas and a small amount of alcohol to the wine. In a fully sparkling wine this is typically about one-and-a-half per cent by volume, so the base wine for a 12 per cent alcohol sparkling wine will have been just 10.5 per cent vol. Underripe, high acid base wines result in the best balance in the finished product.

The tank method

The simplest large-scale method, called the tank method or *cuvée close* in French, was invented in the early part of the twentieth century by a Frenchman called Eugene Charmat. He modified the longwinded and expensive Champagne method, which we will look at next, in order to reduce the cost of production. Still, dry wine is placed in a sealable tank capable of withstanding the pressure of the finished wine. Yeast and sugar are added and the vat sealed so that the gas formed by the second fermentation remains in the vat and dissolves in the wine. The yeast forms a sediment which is removed by bottling the wine under pressure through a filter. The wines are chilled before filtration to help retain as much carbon dioxide as possible and thus maintain the required amount of fizz when the wine is poured.

The *cuvée close* or Charmat method has come in for a great deal of criticism over the years with many commentators claiming that the bubbles are neither as fine, nor as long lived, as in the more expensive methods. There is no scientific evidence at all to suggest that the bubble size is really larger, and the poor general quality is largely to do with the base wine and the way in which the method has been used, rather than the method itself.

Unlike the next two systems we will look at, the tank method does not normally contribute any additional flavours to the wine, so the quality and character of the finished product relies on the quality and style of the base wine. If it is well made from interesting grapes, a high quality bubbly can result. The tank method is particularly suitable for sparkling wines made from aromatic varieties where the flavour of the fruit is able to stand out. Look out for a good German Riesling Sekt to prove this.

The tank method is used widely for inexpensive sparkling wine brands and can usually be identified on the label by what they do not say rather than what they do. 'Vin mousseau' or just sparkling wine, with no other indication of method, is usually, though unfortunately not always, a good clue. Very occasionally you will see the words 'Charmat Method' on the label; perhaps the producer is hoping that the buyer will read 'Charmat' as 'Champagne'.

The Asti method

The frothy wines of Asti (formerly labelled Asti Spumante) in northern Italy are made by their own method, which is often inaccurately considered a variation of the Charmat system. The difference is fundamental. In the Charmat method a still wine is made that is then made sparkling by a second fermentation. In Asti the must never finishes its fermentation, it is never fermented out to dryness. Moscato grapes are picked and pressed but the must is then stored in refrigerated tanks at just below 0°C until needed, at which point it is allowed to warm up and yeast is added. Fermentation initially occurs in tanks that permit the resulting carbon dioxide to escape but when the half-fermented wine reaches about 6 per cent vol the fermentation is halted by further cooling and the wine transferred to tanks that will withstand the pressure of the second fermentation. This second fermentation is encouraged by warming the wine but very shortly afterwards, when the alcohol level is between 7 and 8 per cent, it is halted yet again by chilling and the new wine is bottled through a sterilizing filter under pressure. The result is a lively wine with marked residual sweetness and a peachy, grapey flavour from the Moscato grapes. Similar sweetish sparkling wines are made by the same method in various parts of Italy but are rarely as good as Asti which, despite being unfashionable, can be a delicious glass of wine.

The key to understanding Asti is freshness. Asti is unashamedly light, sweet and tastes of the grapes from which it was made. Unlike many other sparkling wines, Asti does not try to be Champagne; it is itself. Its only problem is that it has a very limited shelf-life, and unless it is drunk young it can taste soapy rather than grapey, lacking the vitality that it should have. Buy your Asti from somewhere you know, where you can ask about the age of the stock and be able to trust the answer you get. All too often the wine is sold too old, by which time it has developed an uninteresting character and becomes just sweet and fizzy.

The traditional method

The traditional method is the new name for the system that has been used in Champagne for centuries. Until recently it was universally known as *Method Champenoise*, or the Champagne Method, but a European Union ruling has forbidden this term in the EU for any wine except Champagne, and as the Champenois have no need to use the term, it has effectively been forced into extinction within the EU. The method was developed in the Champagne region of northern France and involves a second fermentation in the bottle, significantly in the bottle in which we then buy the wine.

A base wine of about 10.5 per cent vol is made, usually by blending a number of different vats in order to achieve the desired flavour, quality and consistency – most sparkling wines at all levels of price and quality are sold as brands, and consumers expect consistency in a brand. This base wine is then bottled with a small amount of yeast and a dose of sugar solution, and the wine is sealed, usually with a crown cap rather than a cork at this stage. The yeast works on the sugar, converting it into alcohol and bubbles that, because the bottle is sealed, have nowhere to go other than to dissolve in the wine.

So far so good. We have a sparkling wine, but we also have a sediment. The yeast, now dead, forms a sticky deposit on the side of the bottle, called the lees. This has to be removed, but not until the wine maker has got some added value out of it. If left in the wine the cell structure of the dead yeast starts to break up, releasing flavours into the wine.

to move the sediment down to the neck of the bottle, sparkling wine bottles are placed in these racks, called purpitre, where they are twisted and moved up through a fraction of an angle until they are nearly vertical, with the next, and the sediment, at the bottom

Once the maturation phase is over the wines have to be cleared of their sediment. Two processes are used. One moves the yeast down the bottle to the cap, the second removes it from the bottle. This process is almost always called *remuage* and was developed by Veuve Clicquot. It involves gradually twisting and tilting the bottles, which are held in specially designed racks called *pupitres*. These hold the bottles by the neck in holes that will allow the bottle to rest at almost any angle between horizontal and nearly vertical, but upside down. Over a number of weeks the bottles are twisted to loosen the sediment and the base lifted to move it down the neck of the bottle. Once in this position the bottles are removed from the racks and the necks dipped in a freezing solution, which forms an ice-plug around the yeast. A machine then returns them to the upright position, and removes the cap, allowing the pressure to force the ice-plug out, leaving the wine clear and sparkling. This is called *dégorgement* or disgorging. The bottles are then topped up and sealed with the final cork. This is inevitably a longwinded and costly process that has been mechanized in various ways.

It is the maturation on the lees that makes the traditional method special, not the much-vaunted *remuage* and *dégorgement*, that makes traditional method wines special, so for the full effect you need to look out for long yeast ageing. The longer the maturation the greater the complexity and intensity. However, it is maturation on the yeast that matters – do not be tempted to keep sparkling wine in your own cellar for too long. Many traditional method sparkling wines, and Champagne in particular, benefit from a few months of post-disgorgement maturation, but keeping them too long can result in hardened corks that fail to keep the wine fresh.

The transfer method

The tank method is cheap, but fails to give the complexity of yeast ageing. The traditional method gives complexity but is expensive. A compromise lies in the transfer method; a hybrid between the two systems that requires huge capital outlay but once the machinery is installed, can produce good wines at a lower price. The process starts the same way as the traditional method but instead of going through the expensive *remuage* and *dégorgement*, the wine is decanted under pressure into a clean bottle. If sufficient time has been allowed for maturation, this method can result in a complex sparkler.

Labelling

There are usually clear clues on the label to indicate which method has been used. Traditional method wines are the easiest to spot – this is an expensive method and so the label will usually boast of it. Many European sparkling wines made in specific areas must be made by the traditional method. All AC sparkling wines, for example, with the exception of Clairette de Die Tradition, and the Spanish sparkling wine, Cava.

Tank method wines, as we have seen, tend not to boast about their origins, so nothing on the label probably indicates a tank method wine. Transfer method wines often have the words 'bottle fermented' somewhere on the label. Without any indication of which bottle assume this means transfer, but if the label says 'fermented in this bottle' the traditional method has been used.

Tasting the method

This tasting is going to require quite a few corks to be popped, so you might want to do it in a group, or rely on very careful notes. ISO glasses are not ideal for sparkling wine so if you have enough champagne flutes or tulip glasses please use them. Do not use the champagne saucer. Once consigned to the history books where it belongs, this atrocious glass is unfortunately regaining popularity and becoming trendy again. Remember to chill the wines well and be careful when opening them, see next page.

Compare the three basic methods by tasting, preferably side by side, a cheap French branded sparkling wine, an inexpensive Australian brand – look for 'bottle fermented' to be sure of a transfer method wine – and a Cava. To make the comparison fair, try to spend about the same amount on each of the last two. Note how the Australian and the Cava have far more of the yeasty, bread, toast, marmite characters that come from lees ageing.

Pay particular attention to the acidity. All good sparkling wines are made from high-acid fruit, which helps the balance in the mouth. Of the three, the Australian will probably have the least obvious because of the riper fruit.

As we saw in light wines, acidity is covered up to a certain extent by sweetness. As most sparkling wines are consumed not with food but on their own at parties and receptions, a bone-dry wine can seem too tart. For this reason most sparkling wine has a little sugar added when the bottles are topped up in traditional method, or just before bottling in the other methods. Look for this when tasting. Even a wine labelled 'Brut' will normally be just off-dry. However, the softer acidity that is found in Cava means that far more of them can be made truly dry.

Different wines, same method

Using the same cheap French sparkling wine as a base wine, compare it to a well-made tank method wine made from more interesting grapes. The branded French sparkling wines are usually made from Ugni Blanc, not that you will be told this on the label because this is one of the world's least interesting grapes. Compare it to a German Riesling Sekt (Sekt is the German term for sparkling wine, it does not mean dry) or one of the many Italian aromatic sparkling wines such as Prosseco di Conegliano-Valdobbiadene. In the first case we have a fairly plain wine whereas in the case of the aromatic wines there is far more to them, but it is the aromatics of the grapes and wine rather than the method that makes them attractive. To see the difference between the tank method and the Asti method try a bottle of Asti alongside any of the above. See how the stopped fermentation retains the grape sweetness and gives a light-alcohol frothy drink.

The effect of grape and climate

Next, look at the traditional method from different parts of the world, and with different ageing. Look to the Cava as your base wine here and compare it to a good, well-known non-vintage (NV) Champagne and Californian sparkling made from Champagne grapes – Pinot Noir, Chardonnay and possibly Pinot Meunier. Many Champagne houses have set up overseas companies making sparkling wine, Moët, Mumm and Roederer are all big Californian interests. It is worthwhile choosing the same maker for the wines from each side of the Atlantic.

Cava is usually made from three native grapes, Macabeo, Xarel-lo and Parellada, and is normally aged on the lees only for the minimum legal requirement of nine months. As a result the final style has far less yeast character than you will find in the other two. (The maturation relies on a process called yeast autolysis, whereby the yeast cells break up in the wine. This does not happen immediately, and some authorities claim that it does not even start for at least six months. Many tasters find it difficult, or even impossible, to taste autolytic flavours in wines with less than 12 to 15 months ageing.)

The other two wines will have had longer ageing. The legal minimum for non-vintage Champagne is 15 months, but this is usually exceeded and most mainstream brands will have had at yeast two years on the lees, as will the Californian example. The differences between these two will show more about the climate than the wine making. Note the extra fruity character of the Californian version, with balanced but not high acidity, compared to more vegetal character of the Champagne, with much crisper acidity, and usually a longer length and fresher finish. The difference here of course is climate – Champagne comes from a cool, marginal climate where the grapes are barley ripe at harvest time, in complete contrast to the sun-drenched vineyards of California.

Notice too, how the two Pinot/Chardonnay blends have a similar basic character beneath the yeast flavours. The crisp, refreshing acidity and citrus flavours of the Chardonnay balance the richness and backbone from the Pinot. The Cava grapes are less intense whether in still or sparkling form, so the resultant wine is more delicate, with refreshing fruit but without the depth of the others.

For a delicate Champagne, look for a Blanc de Blancs. This, on the label, indicates white wine made from white grapes, and in Champagne there is only one white variety. Occasionally you will come across a Blanc de Noirs – made only from the two Pinots.

Opening a sparkling wine bottle

Advanced level comparisons
Having got to grips with the various styles of sparkling wine available, start to think about how the different companies and their wine makers and traditions affect the styles. Select a pair of Australian sparkling wines, one from an entirely local producer such as Yalumba, the other made with the influence of a Champagne house. Both should be traditional method and a similar price. See how much fuller and riper the all-Australian version is, with bigger, sweeter fruit flavours.

Next, start looking at different styles of Champagne.

This is an expensive hobby, but buying a different bottle each week or month is a great deal easier than buying them all together. You will have to rely on detailed and accurate notes to be able to make your comparisons, though. Choose the non-vintage wines from various houses. NV wines are the standard in Champagne – it is these that offer the fairest comparison.

There are dozens of Champagne houses and each is different, each has its own house style. For a real treat, see how a Champagne house's style shows through in different wines. Most Champagne houses make a range of wines, starting at non-vintage, going through vintage and on to at least one, sometime two or more prestige *cuvée* wines. Often there is a rosé NV, and occasionally rosé vintage too, but for the moment let's look at the whites.

You will find the same house style that you described in the last exercise showing through all the wines in the range, but with greater intensity and complexity as a result of the greater yeast ageing and the better quality of the base wine. Note how the fruit is riper too; vintage Champagne is only made in good years, which in this cold, northerly climate, means warm years where the fruit is that much riper at vintage time. The prestige *cuvée* wines will probably also be vintage and will certainly, vintage or not, have had the extra ageing – probably even more than the 'standard' vintage.

The most extravagant Champagne tasting would be a comparison of different prestige *cuvées* – but for this you may need a second mortgage.

Opening sparkling wine
Care is needed when opening a bottle of sparkling wine. Remember that the wine is under pressure and the cork will fly out and may cause injury if not controlled.
Follow the CAT rule:
C – chill the wine. The cooler it is, the more the carbon dioxide stays in solution, thus reducing the pressure.
A – angle the bottle. If you hold the bottle at an angle, the gas can escape when the cork is released without spilling any wine.
T – turn the bottle and hold onto the cork. This gives you better control.
Remember that a loud 'pop' is usually accompanied by wasted wine. A gentle 'phut' usually means no wine will be spilt.

2 fortified wines

Port, Sherry and Madeira can be among the finest wines this planet has to offer. Fortified wines, or liqueur wines as the legislators like to call them, are higher in alcohol than their light wine cousins as a result of having had grape spirit added at some stage during their production, either during fermentation or after it. (It is possible to fortify before fermentation too; this results in a *mistelle*, like the deliciously grapey Pineau de Charente.)

Originally this was the best way of preserving the wines for shipping. In the days before good cellar hygiene wines spoiled all too often and the great triumvirate were able to build their markets and reputations because they were better able to withstand the rigours of shipping. Now with cellar hygiene this is not necessary, but fortification has become part of the style and tradition.

Fashions change and sales of both Madeira and Sherry are lower today than they have been in the past (although Sherry still outsells Port by a very comfortable margin in Britain). Port, by way of contrast, has grown in popularity in both the UK and in North America, the biggest markets for the premium styles, paradoxically for the same reason Sherry sales have fallen – the trend to lighter, lower alcohol drinks. Sherry has been ousted as the dinner party aperitif by white wine, whereas Port has replaced brandy and malt whisky at the other end of the meal. Sadly, fortified wines tend to be overlooked by many wine enthusiasts, relegated to being part of the Christmas fare and ignored for the rest of the year. Yet they offer a wide range of tasting experiences, and are far more versatile than many think. Remember these are wines and, like light wine, should be considered part of the meal, not just an optional extra.

There are a large number of other fortified wines made around the world. In France the tendency is to make sweet fortified either from Muscat, or for red versions, Grénache. The best of these are labelled Vins Doux Naturels (VDN) and in their homeland will normally be served as aperitifs. Italy produces a range of Moscato (Muscat) fortified wines, in particular from Panellaria. Often the local name for the grape, Zibbibo, is used on the labels. Marsala from Sicily, another fortified wine made originally by British merchants, is far more famous. Spain and Portugal make others too – Malaga and Montilla from Spain, Setúbal and the very rare Carcavelos from Portugal have been made for centuries. The New World too has a history of fortified wine production with local equivalents of Port and Sherry once being the mainstay of the wine industries of California, South Africa and Australia. Today these are declining in importance as the light wines dominate the world stage, but Muscats from the Rutherglen area in the Australian state of Victoria is one of the world's classic wine styles, as are the oddly named 'Tokays'.

Making fortified wines

Timing of fortification is the difference between Port and Sherry. Port is sweet because it is fortified during fermentation, when some of the grape sugar remains unfermented. Fortification kills the yeast, preserving natural sweetness. Sherry is fermented to dryness, and then fortified with sweet Sherry being sweetened with specially made sweet wines added to the dry base wine shortly before bottling. Madeira can be made in either method, but with its own special maturation technique. Much of the style of these wines comes from the production and the maturation – grapes, soils and vineyard location are important – but their influence is diluted by the wine's subsequent treatment.

Perhaps the easiest of all fortified wines to understand are the Vins Doux Naturels of southern France. The most famous of these is Muscat de Beaume de Venise from the southern Rhône but there are many other white examples such as Muscat St Jean de Minervois, Muscat de Rivesaltes and Muscat de Frontignan. Red versions also exist with names such as Banyuls and Rasteau, but these are not as easy to find.

As a starting point in fortified wine tasting get hold of bottle of Muscat de Beaume de Venise to taste. You will be familiar with the grapey character of this variety if you have worked your way through the light wine exercises. Note how here it is more intense on the nose because the spirit lifts the flavours out of the glass. Note, too, how the wine clings to the sides of the glass as you swirl it – a sure sign of elevated alcohol. On the palate you will immediately notice the sweetness, balanced here by both acidity and alcohol. This sweetness is the natural sweetness of the grapes, in the case of Muscat de Beaume de Venise, the finer quality Muscat Blanc à Petit Grains, preserved by the addition of pure, clean spirit that kills off the yeast and thereby allows for a stable yet sweet wine.

Sherry

Sherry can only come from Spain, and only from a very carefully defined triangle in Andalucia, in the south of Spain. Here the chalky albariza soil retains the winter rains, allowing the Palomino vine to flourish through the hot dry summer. Palomino, also known as Listan, is a particularly uninteresting grape, responsible for many bottles of dire, neutral, low-acid light wine when grown almost anywhere else.

The must is fermented to dryness, usually in stainless steel these days, and pumped into casks called butts.

Unusually for wine, the butts are not filled, but left 'on ullage' that is with a large air gap at the top. In any other wine this would be disastrous, for Sherry it is essential. After a few months the wines are assessed by the cellar-master, or 'capitaz' and classified. From this day on the wines' futures are mapped out – Sherry gets its differing styles from management of the wines in butt far more than vineyard location. Some wines are rejected. Of those that remain, the finest and most delicate are classified as Fino and fortified to 15.5 per cent vol. The fuller, richer wines are classified to 18 per cent. This is important because there are two possible routes for the wines to follow. Fino butts develop a foamy layer on the surface of the wine. This is flor, a type of yeast that lives on glycerine, alcohol and some acids in the wine while protecting it from oxidation. In so doing it flavours the wine with a unique yeasty, salty flavour, described sometimes as like almonds, or dried apple. The olorosos oxidize in a controlled manner, gaining colour and in time a powerful walnut aroma and rich, full palate – albeit dry.

All Sherry styles are based on these two.

Finos are sold as such, or as Manzanilla if matured in the coastal town of Sanlúcar de Barrameda, where the cooler climate encourages thicker flor growth. Pale cream (and pale Amontillado) are sweetened Finos, sweetened with rectified concentrated grape must.

Oloroso can be bought in its natural dry form, but more often is sweetened with sweet wines made from raisined Pedro Ximinez (PX) grapes and sold as sweet Oloroso, cream or brown. If the flor on a Fino is killed off, either through long ageing or additional spirit, the wine will start to oxidize, becoming not Oloroso, but Amontillado, either sold relatively young and probably sweetened to medium dry, or matured longer and sold as a classic dry Amontillado.

Sherry tasting

As a starting point, try each of the three classic Sherry types: Fino, Amontillado and Oloroso. Buy a dry Amontillado and a dry Oloroso. Try to get equivalent qualities in each case, and do ensure the Fino in particular is a nice fresh example – ask the person behind the counter before you buy, and if they are not sure, buy elsewhere. (For some suppliers you can read the lots number.) The three do not have to be from the same

Sherry house, indeed some Sherry houses specialize in one type of Sherry and others in another. Don't forget to serve the Fino chilled. The other two can be at room temperature in the winter, but you may want to take the excess heat off them if you are tasting on a hot summer day.

Note the colours – this is the first time we have looked at brown wines instead of red, white or pink – but remember that some brown-coloured Sherries are that colour because they have been coloured and/or sweetened with PX. The pale yellow colour of a Fino often comes as a surprise to newcomers to Sherry, if only because of the image of Great Aunt Maud's glass of dark cream at Christmas. Typically the Amontillado will be medium amber in colour, paler than the Oloroso which will be both deeper and more brown than amber. A great deal depends on the brands you choose, though. All of these wines will form distinct tears or legs on the glass

pale colour of a Fino Sherry

Amontillado is deeper because of deliberate oxidation

when swirled – remember this shows nothing more than alcohol.

Nose each of the three. The Fino in particular has a distinctive character that cannot be confused with anything else. What you are smelling is not fruit, or wood, but the effect of flor. Descriptors like yeasty, dried apple, blanched almonds and marzipan come to mind.

The Amontillado might remind you of brown sugar, caramel and nuts, in particular hazelnuts, and the Oloroso will be richer, a fuller and more generous flavour, but again nuts, caramel and sugar.

Taste each in turn. If this is your first taste of Fino, you may be almost shocked by the dryness initially. It is bone dry, with remarkably low acidity, yet is still mouth-watering in a salty sort of way, with the flor character coming through forcefully on the palate. Fino, or in particular Manzanilla, the Fino from Sanlucar de Barrameda, is of course the perfect accompaniment for olives, but as with olives, not everyone will like it on their first encounter.

One final point about Fino. It is usually only 15.5 per cent vol, not much higher than a light wine. Treat it as such – it will still be fine after a day or two in the fridge, but don't keep open bottles for weeks on end.

Fino or Manzanilla with olives is a match made in heaven

If you have bought a good example the Amontillado will be even more concentrated. Still dry and low in acidity, but with a massive nutty palate. This is the first wine we have looked at that has been deliberately oxidized. Note the flavours that result.

The Oloroso should be fuller and richer. It can seem sweeter, even when totally dry, which is why this style is the most popular choice for the sweeter styles of Sherry.

Having tasted the classics, compare them with the more commercially important medium and cream Sherries. A medium will normally be based on an Amontillado, and the cream will be based on Oloroso. See how in both cases the sweeter versions are less concentrated too. This comes from being younger wines – Sherry gains concentration and complexity with long wood ageing but this is not always appropriate for the high-volume brands.

When to drink Sherry

We tend to see Sherry as a pre-dinner drink only, yet in Andalucia it is drunk throughout the meal. Fino is ideal with shellfish, as well as olives, hams etc. Amontillado is great with grilled meats while Oloroso and full-flavoured game is a match made in heaven.

For a real treat, get hold of a bottle of PX Sherry. This is not widely available, the Sherry producers themselves use most of it. It is unctuously sweet, thick and viscous in the glass, varying in colour from dark golden brown to tar-like black treacle. Not a wine you need to drink much of at a sitting, but delicious all the same. This is one wine that can stand up to ice-cream and even the sweetness of treacle tart.

Port

'The first duty of Port is to be red, and the second is to be drunk.' So Ernest Cockburn is reputed to have said. As we will see, there is far more to Port than either ruby or vintage.

Having worked through Sherries, Port tasting will seem far simpler – the distinctions between the different styles are perhaps more straightforward, and the flavour associations are more akin to those found in fruity light wines.

Port is the fortified wine of the Douro Valley in northern Portugal. It is fortified part-way through fermentation

like the VDN. Port is naturally sweet. Variations in sweetness occur because of individual house styles, and the aims of the wine maker rather than natural factors. A whole raft of different local grapes go into its production, with few producers knowing with any certainty exactly what they are working with because in most cases grapes are bought in from dozens of small growers. The vineyards here are among the most difficult in the world – rugged hillside terrain that has to be blasted with dynamite and shaped by bulldozers before vines can even be planted – resulting in vineyards where almost every task has to be carried out by hand. Wine making too can be labour intensive. Because of the arrested fermentation, at which point the skins (source of colour and tannin) are discarded, the extraction has to be both rapid and thorough. The human foot is still considered the best way to make Port, probably the only remaining area in the world where wine is still made commercially in the same fashion as depicted in the tombs of the Pharaohs. Foot-treading is increasingly expensive and today, alongside the stone *lagars*, or troughs, visitors will see stainless steel or concrete vats, and in the most modern wineries, robots being used.

Whatever the extraction and fermentation equipment used, it is the selection and maturation that gives us the different categories of Port. There are only a recognized handful, so it is relatively easy to get to grips with the basics, but of course each house has developed its own house style as well.

A summary of the maturation requirements is listed below, along with the resultant styles, but from a taster's point of view we will start by considering the basic colour first. In simple terms, Port is made in white, red and brown.

White Port

Little white Port is drunk in the UK, but it is very important in the domestic market, and in France (the biggest export market) and the Benelux countries. Most white Port is sold as young, a couple of years after being made, and it should be drunk as fresh as possible. There are two widely available styles – those labelled simply 'white Port', which are as sweet as any other Port, and those labelled 'dry white Port', which are drier but not generally totally dry. Both are sold as aperitif wines, competing with Fino Sherry. They should be light, fruity and fresh, but getting a fresh example is not always easy.

the Douro Valley in northern Portugal is one of the most dramatic vineyard regions in the world

Sales tend to be slow and shop stock can linger on the shelves too long. The only widely available exception to this is Churchill's, which is sold after considerable wood ageing. The result is a wine of far deeper colour, with greater intensity and complexity, a wine that can better stand the slow stock rotation, albeit at a higher price.

Compare the basic types with Fino. Hopefully, you will find them more fruity, and of course sweeter, but without the tang of flor that makes Sherry unique. Consider the affect of the higher alcohol level. At typically 19 or 20 per cent, white Port is noticeably more warming and alcoholic than Fino, even when served chilled, as it should be. White Port is often used as a mixer in its native Douro. After a really hot day, a glass of white Port with plenty of ice and a splash of tonic water is a wonderful restorative.

Red Ports

Ruby, vintage and late bottled vintage (LBV) would be far more to Ernest Cockburn's taste. Most of the grapes grown in the Douro, and certainly the best grapes, are black, so logically the best wines at least start off red.

Ruby – often labelled 'fine ruby' – is the most basic. Light, fruity wines, again sold young for early consumption, these are the bread and butter wines, the bulk of the trade, for most shippers. Made like any other Ports, they will have been selected and blended to give deep colour and lively fresh red and black fruit flavours. What they will generally not have is any great structure – these are wines to be enjoyed in their youth and therefore will not have much tannin.

One level up from basic ruby is the category of reserve. In the past, these were often called 'vintage character', a name that is gradually being phased out for fear of confusion with true vintage Port. These are premium rubies that usually offer far greater taste satisfaction than fine ruby, at only a small price premium.

LBV is marketed as a stepping-stone to vintage. The bottles carry the vintage date but the wine is, as the name says, bottled later – between four and six years from the vintage. Both vintage and bottling dates will appear on the label. There are two fundamental types of LBV, the traditional style that benefits from bottle maturation and the modern style made for immediate consumption; all of the big-selling brands of LBV are in the latter category.

Top of the range in red Ports is vintage. Produced only a few times a decade – typically thrice every ten years for the major Port houses – vintage Port is bottled when young, usually two years from the harvest, in expectation of long bottle maturation. Typically vintage Ports reach their peak between 15 and 20 years after the grapes were picked.

Vintage Port will throw a sediment so it is vital that the wine be decanted, and you should then try to drink it within a few days. These wines have spent their entire life away from air and will tend to oxidize quite quickly once they come into contact with oxygen. The older the vintage, the sooner the decanter should be finished.

Tawny Port

Similarly long maturation, but this time in wood gives us the third category – tawny. True tawny Port is the result of long ageing in old wooden casks – known as pipes – which allow for a long, slow and controlled oxidation. The result is a brown-coloured wine, hence the name, and a very different wine. The dark berry fruit flavours will gradually change to dried fruit – typical of the 10-year-old wines – to nutty, roast almond in particular, spicy character with greater cask ageing.

Look out for a specific age on the label – 10, 20, 30 or over 40 years old are made by most of the big shippers.

young vintage Port is so deep it is almost purple/black in colour, which will fade to ruby with maturity

tawny Port ages in wood so loses its red colour to become tawny, as with this 20-year-old wine

This guarantees the style and a certain level of quality. There are other tawnies with far less specific information on the label. Something labelled 'fine tawny' and selling at the same price as a ruby will be a simple, fruity wine, a little lighter than ruby but in the same mould. 'Old', 'aged' or 'reserve' tawny will all be better, and can be excellent, but without specialist knowledge it is difficult to determine how old and therefore what style the bottle contains.

Port tasting

White Port is well worth considering alongside Sherry, but the rest are worth direct comparison. However, given both the alcohol content of these wines and the cost, you may well want to taste them one at a time and make detailed notes, or, preferably, taste overlapping pairs at a sitting.

First look ruby, or a premium ruby/reserve wine and compare it to an LBV. The Ruby should be very youthful, deep ruby red (if any wine is ruby this should be) with a vibrant fruity nose and palate. It will, of course, be sweet and very high in alcohol. But it will not be complex, neither will it have a great deal of structure – low tannins are the norm. The LBV will have more of everything. It will be deeper, fuller, richer, more complex and with a greater level of tannin – the remnants of the tannin that has allowed the wine to mature for the four to six years that the law requires.

Comparison of the LBV with the vintage is an interesting one, the results of which will vary considerably with the vintage selected. Most Port is matured, blended and sold ready to drink; if the blender is doing his job correctly, the style will not vary much from year to year. Vintage Port, by contrast, varies considerably according to the vintage, and to its age. For this exercise, get hold of a mature vintage, something at least 10, and preferably around 20 years old. Select from one of the famous Port houses. Decant it carefully and then compare it with the LBV.

The first difference will be the colour and in particular the rim. A top vintage Port, even at 20 years old, will still have deep colour, but not as deep, and the rim should by now be broad, beginning to turn garnet. The nose may well be a surprise. Many people expect massive concentration, with flavours leaping out of the glass and almost assaulting the nostrils, but mature vintage is not like that. The wine will be very pronounced, but will have lost the sheer power of the younger wine. In its place you will find myriad layers of different flavours, fruit – both fresh and dried – spice, chocolate, earthiness; this should be one of the most complex of Ports. The tannins will have softened, but will still be there.

Because the LBV is more youthful it can stand being kept a week or two after opening, but you should drink the vintage as soon as you can. The older it is, the sooner it needs to be drunk after decanting.

One of the most instructive Port tastings is the comparison between vintage and aged tawny. Buy a 10 or 20-year-old tawny. It need not be the same shipper as the vintage, but choose one roughly matching the age of the vintage and compare the two. Ideally the tawny should be served slightly chilled. These really are two very different wines, the tawny being, of course, brown in colour, showing nutty and dried fruit characters, low tannin and, although complex, a very different flavour profile.

Madeira

The third great fortified wine is Madeira, all too often ignored, even by aficionados. Madeira comes from an island of the same name in the Atlantic, closer to Morocco than to Portugal, but part of Portugal none the less. Five grapes are cultivated but the varietal characteristics are irrelevant, long since destroyed by the maturation process. When you see a variety on the label, it indicates the basic style: Sercial the driest, usually off-dry, then Verdelho, medium dry; Bual, medium sweet and Malmsey, fully sweet and very rich. The fifth grape, Tinta Negra Mole, is never seen on the label, but the younger, and cheaper Madeiras, labelled just with the style – dry, rich and so on – are all made from it.

What makes Madeira unique is a combination of the viticulture and maturation. Steep, terraced vineyards are covered with high-trained vines on volcanic soil. The soil and shading of the bunches results in very high natural acidity. Once made, the wines are subjected to a unique cooking process called *estufagem*. Here the wines are heated, gently and naturally for the best, artificially and rapidly for the lesser wines. This caramelizes the sugars and gives the wines a very distinct burnt-toffee tang.

Tasting Madeira

As a starting point, choose a Malmsey Madeira, the sweetest style. Go for one with a stated age, as anything without an age statement is likely to be the basic young wine and will lack the real Madeira qualities. It is worth comparing this to the sweet Sherry we tasted earlier in this chapter. Note the distinctive nose, described as toffee, coffee, caramel, toffee-apple or burnt. There is an oriental flavour about the wine, a sweet and sour effect that comes from the high acidity. This is far higher in Madeira than in Sherry.

The aged Madeiras are not cheap, but are well worth the extra expense. To prove it, try your Malmsey with a cheaper Madeira, labelled full, sweet or rich, but without either grape variety or age. The difference is enormous.

The other styles maintain the same tang but are different in sweetness, and because there was less sugar in the wines at the time of *estufagem*, they will all be paler in colour too. Sercial is pale amber, off-dry and with that distinctive tang again. It makes a perfect aperitif, if you are having a full-flavoured starter, and goes very well with soup. Verdelho, being medium, is ideal on its own, whereas the sweeter styles can be drunk after dinner or with nuts and cheese.

all Madeiras, especially the sweeter styles, often smell of freshly-roasted coffee

wine service

Far too many people get overly concerned about wine service. In the rarefied atmosphere of haute cuisine restaurants and silver service, there is a protocol that has developed about the right way to open a bottle, the selection of decanters, the correct way to pour and the right sort of glass. At home, this is excessively fussy but you still have to open the wine, and if you serve there are ways of getting the most out of each glass. In this chapter we will look at opening the bottle, when and how to decant and identifying wine faults.

Corks and stoppers; wine bottle closures

Most wine bottles are sealed with cork. Cork is the bark of a type of oak that thrives in southern Portugal and parts of Spain. The bark is harvested every nine years – without killing the tree – then cleaned and cut into the familiar stopper shape.

A cork works because the cells of the bark are flexible and form little cavities on the surface that stick to the glass of the bottle neck like millions of microscopic sucker pads from a toy bow and arrow. Removing the cork breaks these little vacuum seals, which is why the initial effort required is often the greatest.

Corks are traditional, and will probably never be replaced in the finest of wines. They do, however, occasionally fail. Bacteria can cause a reaction within the cork that results in a foul-smelling musty compound called 2-4-6-trichloroanisole (TCA), better known as corkiness. Many people have tried to estimate the number of corky bottles, sometimes coming up with vastly inflated numbers. One famous wine writer puts the figure at 10 per cent, which is ridiculously high. The biggest and most thorough survey carried out so far, by the Wine and Spirit Association in London, concluded that around 0.7–1.2% of bottles on the UK market were affected which is a lower estimate, but still higher than any of us would like. That means that we should come across one corky bottle in between 84 and 142 bottles we open and a failure rate that should be avoidable with appropriate measures in the cork industry.

The cork industry is trying to improve matters, but in the meantime a number of other closures have come onto the market. Plastic stoppers in all colours are appearing, and screw caps have begun to appear on wines other than the very cheapest. Plastic 'corks' are now widely accepted by the consumer, even though, or perhaps because, they still need a corkscrew to remove them. Screw caps are less accepted at present, but time will tell. After all, most beverages can be opened without an awkward, and sometimes expensive, gadget. Should wine be different?

Corkscrews and opening

Since the advent of the cork inventors have constantly striven for the ideal way of extracting it. The corkscrew itself is a very simple object, but the effort involved in

pulling the cork from the bottle can be considerable, so dozens of different lever and screw systems have been developed to make life easier for the drinker. In addition there are the air pumps that attempt to force the cork out by air pressure in the bottle, Port tongs, sabres for Champagne and the two-pronged butler's friend.

When selecting a corkscrew, look first at the screw itself. Avoid the gimlet type, which are fine for most corks, but will destroy the old and frail corks you will find in older vintages. The longer the screw, the greater purchase it will have on the cork, so go for the longest helix you can find. The American-designed 'Screwpull', and its imitators take it to the ultimate extreme.

Next look at the lever action. Few people now use the simple T-bar, operated with brute force. Try out all the types you can to see what action works best for you. The selection on the next page will help.

Most corkscrews are equipped with foil cutters of some description, either a small knife or the four-wheeled cutter type. The knife type should be used below the neck flange of the bottle so that wine does not drip over the capsule – more important in the past when capsules were made of lead than with today's tin, aluminium or plastic capsules.

the most commonly used corkscrew is the waiters' friend

apart from the basic model variations include slight movement of the fulcrum, the two-step, double-lever and, third in line, the hand-made, ergonomically designed version – expensive but a joy to use

the Screwpull, which comes in various versions, avoids the need to lever the cork by having a long helix that goes all the way through the cork

finally, on the extreme right is the butterfly model, in this case one with the damaging gimlet type of screw

not illustrated are the boxwood corkscrew, which takes the strain out of opening by means of a reverse wooden screw, and the simplest of all, the T-bar, which relies on brute force to extract the cork

Decanting

Crystal decanters look impressive on the table, and are highly collectable in their own right, but there are few occasions today when we really need to use them. The reason for decanting are two-fold: either the wine has thrown a sediment that needs to be removed or it needs to be aerated. This can occur in very tannic, young red wines.

The word decanter implies something quite special, but any clean bottle, carafe or jug will do as long as it holds

at least as much as the original bottle – the last thing you want to do is stop half-way through pouring.

Sediment in wine happens naturally as fine wines mature. Colour, tannin and tartrate crystals form as the wine matures in the bottle. This sediment is totally harmless, but is unsightly in the last glass. To decant a wine that has been lying undisturbed throughout its life, remove it from the rack, place it in a decanting basket, open it, ensuring the neck of the bottle is clean, and pour carefully into the decanter, watching the sediment and stopping before it reaches the neck. A candle, or other light source behind the bottle, is useful here.

If the wine has been disturbed while it matures the sediment will be broken up so it is preferable to leave the bottle standing upright for 12 to 24 hours before decanting to allow the sediment to settle at the bottom of the bottle.

Decanting to aerate wine

Let's get one old wine chestnut out of the way. Opening a bottle of wine to let it aerate for an hour or two before it is drunk, as recommended by some, is utter rubbish. Some wine can benefit from a little aeration, but just pulling the cork leaves a very small surface in contact with the air and there will be no benefit from this. You will get more air into the wine by pouring it into a decanter, or jug, than leaving the bottle open. Young, tannic wines can be opened up, releasing more of their flavour, but beware of old, fragile reds – decant these carefully very shortly before serving to avoid oxidation.

Wine faults

As we have seen, wines are occasionally faulty. Old books on the subject list dozens of possible faults, but modern cellar hygiene and better quality control have assuaged the need to discuss most of these.

Corky wine

Today the most common fault is corkiness, or mustiness. This can be caused by many factors, including wood treatments in the winery or contamination from other storage or packaging material, but the most common cause still appears to be faulty corks. We have all drunk corky wines, only a minute proportion of all wines are ever returned, but as we have seen a far higher number are tainted.

The main chemical responsible is TCA, which can be detected in minute concentrations. It manifests itself in different ways depending on the level present. In small amounts it kills the flavour, making what might be a lively and flavoursome wine seem flat and dull. In greater concentrations, it has a distinctive smell reminiscent of chlorine, or of cork. It is sometimes described as old rotten wood, or damp – as in a room suffering from

damp. It happens randomly, so it may be just one bottle in the case, or it may be more. Try another bottle of the same, it might be fine.

Do remember that a piece of cork floating in the glass is not a sign of corkiness. Neither is corkiness a catchall terms for wine faults, it has a very specific meaning.

Oxidation

Less common but still a major problem is oxidation. If the wine is too old, and particularly if the cork has failed, air will react with the wine, turning it more brown and killing the flavour, replacing it with a dull, flat nose and taste. It is often described as tasting of Sherry. Oxidation is avoidable by the wine maker using the correct dose of sulphur dioxide, by correct storage, and by drinking the wine within the expected shelf-life.

Oxidation is usually a simple chemical reaction. If bacteria and air are allowed to combine in the wine, you may get volatility. Here acetic acid bacteria convert alcohol into vinegar, known in wine-making circles as volatile acidity or VA. A small amount of VA is present in all wines, and elevated levels are common in such wines as Barolo and Madeira, but in excess, the wine becomes undrinkable.

Excess sulphur dioxide

Sulphur dioxide is a vital part of wine making. It acts as an antiseptic, killing the bacteria that cause volatility, and as a sponge to mop up excess oxygen thus preventing oxidation. It must, however, be used with caution. Sulphur dioxide is a highly poisonous gas, so strict rules apply in the winery, and these extend to legally enforced limits in the final wine. Some people, however, are particularly sensitive to it. If you find yourself sneezing when nosing your glass or if you get a painful grip in the nasal cavity, rather like getting your nose too close to the smoke just as a match is struck, that is caused by excess SO_2. This is one fault that you can deal with yourself, by giving the wine a good shake in the glass. The SO_2 will react with the air and disappear.

All wine faults are preventable, but not all wine faults are curable. They make the product undrinkable, and therefore unsuitable for the purpose. If you bought a television that didn't work you would return it. Whatever the fault, affected wines should be returned to the supplier for a replacement or refund.

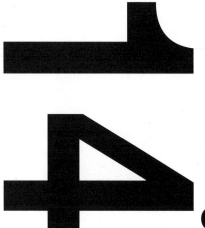

glassware

As we saw in the early chapters, most tasters use the ISO glass when working, and I strongly recommend that you use it when studying wine, partly because of the design, partly for consistency of results. However, although it is an indispensable tool for the taster, it is not the most attractive of drinking vessels. The chances are that you will want to open your best wines with friends over dinner with an attractive table setting, and that will, inevitably, include smart glassware. When something grand is called for, to add to the sense of occasion, the ISO will just not do.

A brief trip to any department store will show how glass manufacturers are falling over themselves to supply, and indeed create, a market for all sorts of different styles. Different shapes and sizes, colours and cuts. Plain glass, patterned glass, cut glass, moulded glass; but which to choose? Here we will look at the effect different glass shapes have on wine so we can build up a list of glass dos and don'ts for when the time comes to invest in a new set.

For this exercise you are going to need to go hunting, begging and borrowing. You will need to get hold of as many different types and shapes of glass as you possibly can. You will probably have a selection around the home anyway – your normal wine glass, the ISOs you have been using for the other parts of the course, a tumbler and an old-fashioned glass; perhaps old Sherry glass, or liqueur glasses. You may well have a range of elegant glasses that you use for formal occasions; include these too. If you have friends with different glasses, invite them along, or raid the sideboards of elderly relatives to find

different shapes and sizes. Ideally your collection will include most of the standard shapes, such as the Paris goblet, the Elgin Sherry glass, and a range of larger and appropriately shaped drinking vessels.

the ISO glass, the professional's tool

There are no specifications as to which wine you should use for this, just that you should try the same wine from each glass in turn. Using the guidance outlined in Chapter 1, try to taste the wine from each glass, using as close to a standard five centilitre measure as you can manage.

You will find that in some of the smaller glasses the essential swilling is all but impossible, especially in the Elgin or small liqueur glass. Notice too that in both the Elgin and in many straight-sided glasses, assessing the appearance is all but impossible, because the wine spills over the edge of the glass. Swilling wine in the straight glasses can be problematical too.

A standard tasting measure will look very mean in the bottom of a Paris goblet, and will hardly seem to wet the sides of the largest wine glasses on the market. This has implications for swilling, too, of course.

You will almost certainly find that not only is it easier to taste wine from some glasses than others, but that the same wine smells and tastes different, with some of the glasses emphasizing tannin, while others direct the wine to the sides of the mouth where acidity is detected. As a generalization, you will probably find that the best glass is one that has enough space to move the wine around, tapers in towards the top, and is as large as possible, without being too big to be handled easily.

If you went through the same process with a significantly different wine, you would probably come to the same general conclusion, but the best glass for that wine may well be different.

The ISO is a good compromise solution for tasting, and using the same shape of glass for all tasting is recommended for any student of wine. As you can imagine after the last exercise, changing glasses just before a tasting examination would be a disaster.

But no glass is perfect for the enjoyment, as distinct from analysis, of every wine. Sparkling wines need greater height and narrower girth to show off their bubbles – in Champagne you will always be served the wine in a tulip- or flute-shaped glass, never anything rounder, and certainly never the saucer-shaped glasses seen in old Hollywood films.

Glasses recommended for white wine tend to be smaller than those for red. This is because white wines, being

more aromatic, tend to show themselves more easily, and being served when younger will not develop in the glass in the way old reds do. Another consideration is temperature. Wine warms up in the glass, so having a small glass, regularly topped up, means the bottle can be kept chilled, and the diner will get the wine at a more appropriate temperature.

Red wines, especially old and complex examples, therefore, should be served in the largest glasses, with young reds being served in a size between the white and older red.

To my mind the ideal glass for most types of fortified wines is the ISO. In Jerez, Sherry is served in the smaller, but similar shaped, *copita*, but this is to keep the wine in peak condition. There will usually be a bottle of Fino in the ice-bucket near by. In cooler climates the wine should not warm up too fast in the glass.

To have such a range of glasses requires investment in time and money, so most of us will happily compromise on one or maybe two sizes of glass, perhaps an everyday, dishwasher-safe and fairly tough one and something finer for when important guests arrive. If you really want to splash out, however, investigate the Riedel range. This Austrian wine glass maker has developed a massive range of glasses which attempt to provide the ideal glass for every wine. Included in the range is a white Bordeaux, a young red Bordeaux, an old red Bordeaux, red Burgundy, etc. even different glasses for different types of Port. The glasses are a joy to use, but to get the full set would require a second mortgage.

Care of your wine glasses

It is also worth considering the care of glasses. Apart from the obvious risk of breakage, the way you treat your glasses can affect the way you taste your wine. We saw in Chapter 1 how the appearance and smell are important when assessing any wine – and, of course, the same is true when drinking wine. Glasses should be clean and polished to get the best out of them, but you need to take care with how this is done. Detergent of any type has some smell, which is normally very difficult to rinse off, and it kills all the bubbles in sparkling wine. If you want to make a glass of Champagne look like a still wine, wash your glasses in washing-up liquid first. For general care, unless you have to deal with dinner party finger-marks or traces of lipstick, it is best to use hot water only.

Be careful also when using dishwashers. Although the rinse cycle normally removes most of the smell of the detergent, the washing process can damage the surface of the glass. Some glass is harder than others, and some is dishwasher-safe, but other types, particularly lead crystal, which most people consider to be the best, will be scratched horribly if habitually washed by machine.

Tea-towels can also leave their mark. All those fresh 'clean mountain air' smells that manufacturers spend a fortune researching may be welcome in sheets and sweaters, less so in our wines. Fabric softener in the wash is best avoided. Tea-towels also carry food aromas. If you have just washed and dried the crockery from a spicy meal the tea-towel will smell, however imperceptibly, of spice. You may not notice this, but you will if you subsequently use the tea-towel on your glasses and then taste wine with them. Ideally reserve one tea-towel for glasses only.

temperature and tasting

We have all heard or read about the 'rules' for wine service, they are even printed on the back labels of many wines these days. There are long-held views about the 'correct' serving temperatures for wines, leading to rules that unnecessarily worry far too many wine consumers and have led to a vast market in weird and wonderful gadgets that wine lovers can buy to ensure that the temperature is 'right'. Behind all the fuss there is one good reason: wine does taste different at different temperatures. The standard rules are reds at room temperature, whites chilled. It is often recommended that sparkling wine and sweeter whites should be served colder than dry whites. In the case of sparkling, this is for safety reasons – see Chapter 11 – and in the case of sweet wines to help with balance.

However, even these simple rules need a little explanation and expansion. They have been quoted, often it seems without thought, for decades, perhaps for over a century. Remember that 'room temperature' in today's temperature-controlled houses is not the same as it was in the draughty baronial halls of yore. Today we have central heating and double glazing so that even in the coldest parts of the world we walk around in shirtsleeves in the winter (compare that to outfits worn by our Victorian ancestors). Conversely, the homes, offices and restaurants in the tropics are air conditioned to the extent that business suits become *de rigueur* for comfort as much as appearance.

Similarly, chilling facilities now are far more widespread and efficient than ever in the past. Most homes have both refrigerator and freezer and we think nothing of shopping for a week, buying things that previous generations had to buy fresh each day because there was no way of keeping them.

So what do we mean by room temperature, or by chilled?

The room temperature in the rules means, by today's standards, a cool room, one where a man wearing a jacket and tie, perhaps even a waistcoat, would not feel excessively hot. Chilled means cool; it does not mean frozen. The following exercise is designed to demonstrate the effect of temperature on the taste of wine.

In this section we will explore our own reactions to different temperatures for both red and white wines to see what validity the standard rules have, and how they came to be promulgated in the first place.

Tasting and temperature

This exercise can easily be divided into two sessions. For each session you will need:

- Three small bottles with a capacity of no more than 25cl (one-third of a bottle.) Ideally use food-grade plastic such as the PET bottles used for soft drinks. Glass is acceptable if you are careful, but clean plastic will be safer, for reasons we will see shortly.

- Either one red wine or one white, depending on the session.

- Three tasting glasses.

Ideally the white should have crisp acidity, and be aromatic. A young Sauvignon Blanc from New Zealand or Chile would work well. The red should be high in both tannin and acidity. Barolo, Barbaresco or any other Nebiollo-based Piemontese wine will be ideal.

If possible, arrange for a like-minded accomplice to set things up for you so you can taste the wines without knowing which is which.

Check to make sure that the wine is healthy, and then divide each bottle into three, using the 25cl PET bottles.

We will look at the two wines separately.

White wine serving temperatures

Keep one white sample at room temperature, chill one in a normal domestic fridge for about an hour, and put the third sample in the freezing section of a fridge or a deep freeze for about two hours. Keep an eye on this one; you do not want it to freeze solid, hence using PET bottles in preference to glass.

After this time, taste each, ideally without knowing which is which. Compare the flavours and their intensities, and think about how the structure comes across, making full notes of course. We will look at these notes in a moment.

Red wine serving temperatures

Put one red wine in the fridge for a couple of hours, stand another in a bowl of water that is warm to the touch, and leave the other at room temperature.

Again, taste the three wines side by side, compare the characters and make your notes.

Conclusions

Whites

As we saw earlier, the flavour of wine comes through the aromatic components and these tend to be subdued by chilling. As a result the room temperature example will have been the most aromatic, and perhaps even a little oily in character with the most obvious nose. The over-chilled example will probably have been very pleasant, but totally lacking in any aromatic character, with the normally chilled version exhibiting everything you would have expected.

You will probably have found that the whites were all very drinkable, but different palate features came to the fore. Acidity is generally emphasized by chilling, so the room-temperature wine may well have seemed richer and fuller than the others, through appearing to have less acidity. The crispness of the chilled wines will have made them more refreshing and therefore more appealing. If you do this experiment with a group you will probably find that many people prefer the over-chilled wine for this reason.

Reds

The Barolos will probably have been far more obviously different. The chilled red will smell alarmingly dumb, smelling of almost nothing, giving no hint of the usual flavours, while the warm wine will probably seem either riper and fruitier, or cooked and jammy, depending on the wine and the temperature.

The big difference, though, is on the palate. The warm wine will, as for the nose, seem jammy and over-alcoholic, having lost the balance you would have expected. The cold wine will be astringent, very unpalatable with harsh tannins and marked acidity. Again, the chilling has emphasized the acidity, as in the white wines, but this time it has also emphasized the tannins, while suppressing the fruit. The result is a horribly out-of-balance wine.

Tip: This exercise works very well if the wines are served blind, for example if you don't know what the wine is, but also if you don't know that all three are the same in each flight, so if you can get your accomplice to play this game unannounced, so much the better. If you try this with a few friends, pour their wines for them as the temperature of the bottles will alert them to your trickery. If you pour into coloured glasses you could probably persuade your friends that each glass contains a different wine.

wine production

Wine production can be divided into two distinct parts, grape growing, or viticulture, and wine making, turning those grapes into wine, called vinification. The two functions can, and often are, carried out by the same person, but can also be separate, with the grape grower being a fruit farmer supplying the raw material to a winery at a certain price per kilo of grapes.

In the twenty-first century we are blessed with great knowledge about the biological mechanisms that go to make wine. As a result there is no excuse whatever for anyone to make faulty wine. With all the knowledge, both scientific and empirical, gleaned over millennia, most of the possible mistakes have already been made. In the past a wine maker learnt the craft from the previous generation; talking to a friend in the village or the next town would hopefully solve problems when they occurred. Nowadays a typical wine maker is a technocrat, with a degree in the subject and a world of experience available, published in a host of industry journals, and transmitted around the globe both on paper and electronically.

The result is a higher standard at the basic level. Even 15 or 20 years ago wine faults that now would be seen as totally unacceptable were commonplace. Having said that, the majority of today's wine will not excite. Recipe wine making has led to a sameness, with wines from different regions all tasting more and more alike, especially at the cheaper end of the market. The quality may be consistently higher, but in most cases it is not fine. Truly great wine of course requires a good vineyard site, good grapes, but most of all passion from the wine maker.

Wine is a fermented, and therefore alcoholic, beverage. The European Union definition is:

Wine is the product obtained from the total or partial alcoholic fermentation of fresh grapes, whether or not crushed, or of grape must.

This does not even include the word 'drink' or 'beverage' but it is a practical working definition for the legislators which completely fails to grab the attention of the wine enthusiast. If you have worked through even a fraction of the tastings in this book, you will know how great the range and diversity of wines is; myriad flavours available from the smallest wine shop. This chapter will describe how wine is made, and attempt to explain part of the reason for that range of flavours.

The final style and taste of any wine will depend on where and how the grapes were grown, a broad subject encompassing climate, weather, soil and fruit farming, and how the resulting grapes are turned into wine, both the wine making itself and the subsequent maturation.

Grape growing/viticulture

Grape varieties

Nearly all wines are made from grapes of the same species, *Vitis vinifera*. Notable exceptions are many of the wines from New York State; Vidal; and a handful of other varieties in Canada; and a handful of varieties grown in very cool vineyard areas, such as England, where it is sensible for growers to choose specific hybrids that ripen early.

The varieties that we see on labels are just the tip of the iceberg. Even quite knowledgeable wine drinkers might be able to name a dozen or so varieties, probably not many more, yet there are over 3,000 varieties known to be cultivated for wine. The total number is increasing all the time as new crossings come on stream.

Climate and weather

The wine-producing varieties of grape do not grow all over the world. As a rough guide, their limit is between 30 and 50° north and south of the equator. Within these bands there is generally sufficient sun and rain for the vine to produce a good crop. Outside these limits it is either too cold for the grapes to ripen, or, conversely, too hot for the grapes to make good quality wine. There are exceptions to this. Vineyards exist in England and Wales, and even in Sweden, well outside the 50th parallel, and there are vineyards in India, Zimbabwe and Thailand, but it is far more difficult to make fine wine in these areas and very special conditions apply.

most vines are trained along wires in hedges to ease vineyard work

White grapes will ripen with less sunshine than black grapes, and natural acidity is vital to the structure of the wine. The best white wines, therefore, tend to be made in cooler areas, whereas the most satisfying reds tend to come from warmer districts. Countries such as Germany and New Zealand make best use of their cooler climates to produce racy, fresh wines. In warmer countries, cool areas will be sought, for example Yarra Valley in Australia, or Somontano in Spain. Hotter areas will certainly allow white grapes to ripen, but the resulting wines will lack finesse.

many hotter areas still have free-standing bush-trained vines like these in Rioja

Red wines from hot areas such as Barossa in Australia and Rioja in Spain tend to be the ones that grab the headlines. Bordeaux and Burgundy are really at the climate limit for reliable fine red wine production – most reds produced further north are light, fruity and pleasant, but not serious wines. Saying that, some red wines are from areas that are not too hot can be equally good. Some tempering influence on the climate helps add finesse and elegance – the sea influence in Bordeaux, ocean fogs in Napa Valley or the Mistral in the Northern Rhône all contribute to the wines' greatness.

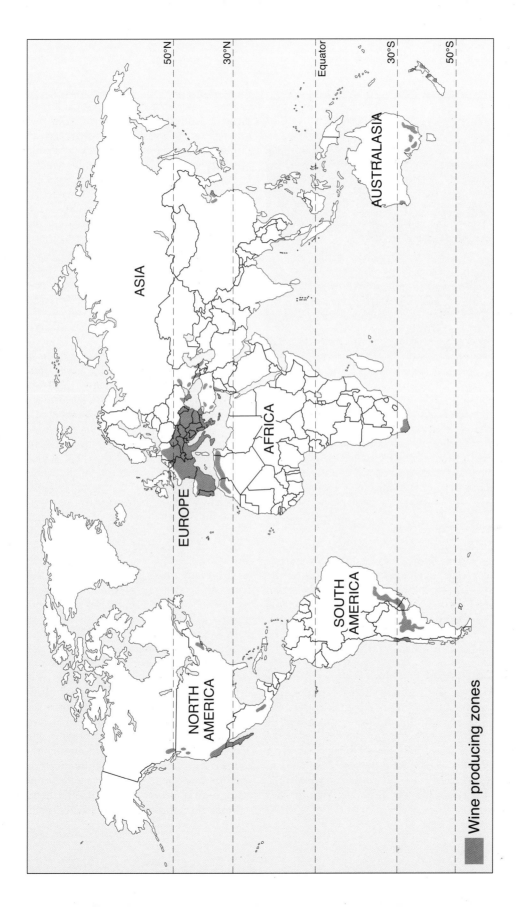

ASIA

EUROPE

AFRICA

AUSTRALASIA

NORTH
AMERICA

SOUTH
AMERICA

50°N

30°N

Equator

30°S

50°S

Wine producing zones

in cool areas, hillside vineyards often yield the best wines

Weather is different from climate. The climate of a given area is fixed, changing only very slowly over time. Weather varies from day to day. The importance of weather is greatest in the more marginal areas where the difference between good and bad years is usually entirely due to the weather pattern during the vine's growth cycle.

Viticulture

All the natural advantages of even the best site mean nothing if the vineyard is badly managed. Only if care is taken at all stages of the vineyard calendar does the grower stand a chance of producing perfect grapes. Even then, viticulture is a gamble. As with all agriculture, the viticulturalist can suffer from the vagaries of the weather. One night of frost in spring, a bad summer hail storm or rain at vintage time can destroy a year's crop.

Wine's quality is determined in the vineyard. Without good raw material, in the form of perfect grapes, the wine makers cannot make good wine. Ideally, and assuming the weather conditions are fine, grapes will be harvested when they are suitable for the style of wine being produced. For crisp, neutral whites, just ripe, totally healthy grapes are needed. As we have seen in Chapter 7, for top sweet wines such as Sauternes the growers are looking for grapes shrivelled by rot and covered in mould.

Assuming the best in vineyard management, the best grapes come from top vineyards. The distance between a basic commune level vineyard in Burgundy, and the greatest of the Grand Crus (great growths or great wines) might be only a few yards, yet the difference in the wines is as great as that between a BigMac and haute cuisine. Climatically the vineyards are identical, the grape variety might be the same, the difference is in the 'terroir'. Simplistically translated as 'the soil', terroir encompasses the soil's chemical composition, its physical formation, and its aspect – altitude and exposure to the sun can have a dramatic effect on the ripeness of the grapes, or their susceptibility to disease. The grower can control these to a certain extent by training the vine in particular ways or by managing the pruning and spraying programmes effectively, but ultimately the factor governing the maximum quality of the grape is inherent in the vineyard.

The most individual wines come from specific, often very small, vineyards. Indeed, the whole appellation contrôlée hierarchy in France, especially in Burgundy, is based on this premise. To blend wines from more than one plot is seen as dilution of the character of the wine. In other areas, where rules are less uncompromising, wine makers have the facility to blend from different vineyards, often many miles apart. For the best wines this is done to improve quality, not diminish it. Prime, complementary parcels of wine from a range of terroirs will be assembled to make a blend better than any one of the individual parts. This is the essence of Champagne making, where all the best wines are a careful cuvée of many different parcels of base wine.

In still wine areas, however, most of the best wines come from single vineyards; some recognized as above average for decades or even centuries. It is often difficult to define exactly what it is that makes a particular piece of land better than its neighbours. Hillsides have been known to produce better wines since Virgil was writing on the subject ('bacchus amat colles'). The additional exposure to the sun will help ripen grapes in cooler areas, whereas in hotter climates, the additional altitude will keep the grapes a little cooler. The structure of the soil will help. Vines prefer well-drained soil so stones, slate and chalk are preferred, and clay positively avoided. Poor soils reduce the yield, while encouraging the roots to search deeper for nutrients. This limits the volume produced but quality and quantity are inversely proportional – all else being equal, fewer grapes means better wine. For this reason too the vineyard owner will limit the yield through severe pruning, and even thinning the crop, removing a proportion of the bunches half-way through the season, encouraging the vine to concentrate its efforts on the remaining crop.

Harvesting and vinification

Whatever style of wine is being made, the choice of the moment of picking is paramount. Grapes must be ripe; how ripe will vary from wine to wine. As grapes ripen on the vine photosynthesis produces sugars that accumulate in the berries. At the same time the natural acids in the berries diminishes. It is easy to measure the ripeness of the grapes by measuring the density of the juice within them, a task often carried out in the field with a simple optical device, the refractometer. For dry wines, care must be taken not to allow the grapes to become overripe, otherwise the wines might lack the essential acidity, or the grapes might start to rot.

Sugar and acid levels are easy to measure and give an objective, scientific definition of maturity. In addition, quality-conscious wine makers all over the world are increasingly returning to what may seem a very unscientific method, tasting the grapes. There is more to fine wine than just alcohol and acid, wine makers are looking for ripeness of flavours too, phenolic ripeness. Research in Australia is leading the way, but to date no computer has been programmed to have a palate. Wines such as Mosel Riesling Kabinetts, bursting with flavour yet only 7 per cent alcohol, are proof that high grape sugar levels are not everything.

half-way through the season black grapes begin to take on colour and accumulate sugar – a stage called 'varraison'

hand picking is back-breaking work, but it is flexible, if slow

machine harvesting is faster and for large vineyards, cheaper, but it can only be done when the vineyard is fairly flat

Harvesting manually has always been a back-breaking job. Teams of pickers comb the vineyards, snipping with secateurs, or hooking the bunches with curved blades like miniature sabres, gathering the fruit in buckets and baskets, emptying these in turn into the hods that transport the grapes to the crusher. Hand picking is slow, and increasingly expensive. Each year it is more and more difficult to find enough workers willing to suffer such pains and discomfort, all for the sake of a minimum wage and a bed in a dormitory, even if the evening meal is hearty, and the wine flows freely.

When hand picking, terrain is not a problem, even the steepest slopes are manageable, but the greatest advantage of hand harvesting is selection. Not every bunch of grapes is perfect, some will be underripe, others affected by rot or mildew. Trained pickers know to discard these, favouring only the perfect bunches. Alternatively, as we have seen, for certain types of sweet wine only rotten berries will be selected. Pickers might go through the vineyard five or six times, each time looking at each bunch but picking only those affected by noble rot.

Machines are now used wherever the topography, wine style and economics permit. Mechanical grape harvesters straddle the rows of vines while motorized beaters shake the branches so vigorously that the berries are torn from the vine. Quick, efficient and a godsend if the weather threatens to turn bad, mechanically harvesting is only economical for large vineyards or where a group of growers can share the enormous cost of the machine. No selection is possible, but where the climate is warm and dry, and vineyard husbandry up to scratch, very high quality wines can result.

Winemaking

There is an old saying in wine making that you cannot make good wine from poor grapes, but you can make poor wine from good grapes. The quality of the grapes is set before the harvest, the potential is there in the berries. All a wine maker can do is preserve that quality, perhaps making up for an occasional deficiency of structure, but not improving the flavour.

Once harvested the grapes need to be processed rapidly. Wine is a natural product, but if nature were left to take its course the grape juice would turn first to wine, then vinegar and ultimately back to water. For wine to be made effectively, the fermentation process must be monitored and controlled. Many options are available to the wine maker at each stage; a finished wine's style and quality will result from decisions made at each stage of the wine-making process. The skill in vinification is choosing which route to take – a wrong turn and some of that potential quality will be lost. We cannot investigate every possible route here, but we will look at the main ways the wine maker influences the final style.

Wine cannot be made to a standard recipe. Typically the raw material, the grapes, will vary in ripeness and acidity levels from vintage to vintage. Yields can vary enormously, putting a strain on winery management, and fashions change from year to year, so what sold well last year might bomb this time. Consider too that a wine maker has only one chance with each batch of grapes, and each vineyard will produce grapes only once a year. For many, a lifetime's experience might only be a few dozen vintages; no wonder so many are choosing to work in both the northern and southern hemispheres. It can double their experience.

White wine making

White wine is, perhaps, the simplest of all wines to make so we will start with white, and then look at red wine making.

White wine is simply the fermented juice of the grape. For white wines only the juice is needed, in red wine making the oenologist is concerned with the extraction of colour from the skins. For the white wine maker the emphasis is on preserving the often delicate flavours of the grape. Gentle handling and cool temperatures are *de rigueur* if the wine is not to become flabby and uninteresting.

Because the skins are generally not needed for white wine making, the first stage is to separate the juice from the skins, stalks and grape pulp. When the grapes arrive at the winery they will be run between rubber rollers set just less than a grape's diameter apart to be crushed, gently breaking the skins without damaging the pips, which contain bitter oils.

A great deal of recent research has shown that many of the aromatic components in white wines are in the area just below the surface of the skin, so wine makers are increasingly turning to skin contact even for white wines from grapes such as Sauvignon Blanc.

With or without skin contact, the grapes are then pressed. For white wine soft, gentle pressing is preferred. Presses come in all shapes and sizes, but today the favoured design is the tank press which uses gentle pneumatic pressure to extract the juice within a stainless steel tank that can be pre-filled with nitrogen to avoid any oxidation of the must. The free-run juice, released by the crusher or from loading the press, is the most delicate, with the finest flavours. As pressing progresses more bitter flavours can be extracted from the skins, so

the finest wines are made from the first pressings and the free-run. At this stage the must is green-yellow in colour and opaque, full of debris from the grapes. It will need to be at least partially clarified before fermentation.

The must is placed in refrigerated vats and left to cold settle overnight. This is gentle and the preferred method for the non-interventionist oenologist, but commercial pressures mean that many cheaper wines, made in bulk, are centrifuged for speed.

Once clear, the must can be fermented. Yeast, or more pedantically, enzymes within yeast, convert the sugar in the must into alcohol and at the same time a whole host of other complex chemical reactions turn the simple grapey flavour of must into the far more interesting flavours of wine. Yeast can be the indigenous micro-flora of the vineyards and winery or may be inoculated using one of many commercially cultivated yeast strains that offer greater reliability.

Cool temperatures are required to preserve the flavour of the grapes. Fermentation is naturally exothermic, that is the reactions release heat that has to be controlled, so the vats are cooled with running water to maintain a temperature of between 10 and 18°C. A higher temperature will speed up the biochemical reactions so the fermentation will be quicker, increasing the wineries'

most modern wineries are equipped with stainless steel tanks for fermentation and storage

productivity, but aromatic components in the must will be lost through evaporation.

Temperatures have to be controlled, but must not drop too low. Very cold conditions, a natural hazard in some wineries, can result in stuck fermentations. More common is the development of bubble-gum aromas that mask the fruit if the fermentation is carried out too cold.

The majority of wines are fermented in inert vats. Large vats of old wood, stainless steel or lined concrete can be seen in wineries throughout the world. The difference between these types of vat is more to do with ease of use than wine quality. A new winery would probably choose stainless steel as a matter of course, but an existing concrete or wooden vat can be just as serviceable, if more difficult to maintain. Ideal for aromatic varieties such as Riesling or Muscat, these vessels do not contribute any additional flavours to the wine.

At the moment oak is the flavour of the month. To get the full effect of oak many wine makers are turning back to

temperature-controlled fermenting vats

barrel fermentation. This was, and always has been, the traditional way of making wine in Burgundy, but in other areas the practice all but died out because of the extra costs involved. Fashion in wine, like anything else, is fickle, and what was outdated 20 years ago is this week's innovation, what was once rare and specialist has become flavour of the month. Suddenly 'barrel fermented' or 'barrique fermented' are appearing on labels from all four corners of the world. As we saw Chapter 5, the important point here is the newness of the wood. Barrels only have a finite amount of the oaky flavours, particularly the vanillin, within them. Fermenting in barrels extracts these faster than static maturation so a barrel can only be effectively used for barrel fermentation a few times before it becomes a small and inconvenient inert vessel.

Many different oaks are used in wine making. The most popular are French, either from the forests of Allier or Nevers, and American. American forests are warmer than the central French ones, so the latter have a finer grain. Furthermore, the American oak is usually sawn, whereas French oak is split. The net result is that American oak gives more obvious vanilla and smoky oak flavours to any wine fermented or stored in it. French oak is considerably more expensive than American, another factor for the wine maker to bear in mind.

Many wine drinkers associate oak flavours with high quality, creating a demand for them in an ever-increasing range of wines. Inevitably this search has led to cheaper alternatives. Barrels are expensive to buy and costly to use because of the extra labour involved in filling a large number of small containers, and in maintaining adequate fill levels thereafter. These days much of the oaky wine seen in the world has got its oak flavour from oak chips, or powdered oak in a sort of overgrown teabag, or oak staves suspended in a stainless steel vat. These methods give the oak flavours that the modern consumer and wine journalist seem to want, without the extra cost. Such additions do come at a price, though, you get the oak without the extra maturity and complexity. They have their place, but never for the finest. Here real barrels are still the norm.

Red and rosé wine making

The biggest difference between red and white wine making is the skins. Nearly all wine grapes have green

old casks, like these Port pipes, do not contribute oaky flavour but add complexity through a small amount of controlled oxidation

pulp, even the deepest of black grapes looks just like a white grape when peeled. All the colour and tannin in red wine comes from the skins so fermentation has to be in contact with the skins. The grapes are therefore crushed, then fermented and then pressed, whereas with whites it is crush, press, ferment.

Colour and tannin are extracted more efficiently at higher temperatures, so red wine tends to be fermented at a higher temperature than white, anything up to 30 or 32°C. As fermentation progresses, carbon dioxide is released which tends to raise the skins to the top of the vat, forming a cap. This has to be worked back into the wine if the extraction is going to occur. Modern wineries usually take clear must from the base of the vat and pump it over the cap. In the past the best way of keeping the cap submerged was to climb into the vat and push it down by foot – a process still used for the finest Ports.

After fermentation, or in the case of rosé, once the required colour is extracted, the wine is run off and the skins, still full of wine, are pressed. This press wine has a higher concentration of colour and tannin than the free-run, but can be too tannic and therefore bitter. It may or may not be blended back into the main wine.

Usually colour is extracted first, followed by tannin, so for light red wines such as Valpolicella the maceration period might be a matter of a few days. For classic, full-structured reds intended for long ageing, the skins might be left in contact with the wine for two or even three weeks.

Maceration carbonique

Carbonic maceration, or *maceration carbonique,* is a technique used to extract colour with very little tannin. Instead of yeast, it relies on intracellular enzymes to start the fermentation. These only work in a carbon dioxide atmosphere, so the vats are flushed out with CO_2 before the grapes, which must be undamaged and still on their bunches, are placed in them. The initial fermentation occurs within the berries, which eventually collapse. At this point the grapes are pressed and fermentation continues as for white wine. *Maceration carbonique* is most famously used for Beaujolais.

Thermovinification

Heat breaks up the cellular structure of the grapes' skins and can be used to help release the colour and tannin. It is not a technique that many producers admit to using as it can, if not used carefully, result in cooked, jammy flavours in the wine. However, there are one or two very famous and prestigious properties that use it. As with anything else, it is how carefully it is used that matters.

Maturation and finishing

All wines spend some time maturing before being bottled. Whether this is a matter of a few weeks in inert tanks, or an extended period in barrel and bottle, eventually the wines will be blended and bottled. Blending is a normal practice for all wines. Even a single vineyard may produce a range of qualities, and different barrels will behave differently. The final act of the fine wine maker then is to select only the best parcels, those that will marry together well, and blend them to make the finished wine. After filtration and stabilization, all that remains to do is bottling.

Winemaking adjustments

Certain basic components of a wine's structure can, quite legitimately, be adjusted by the wine maker to make up for any inconsistencies or deficiencies in the must. These adjustments are best done before fermentation. Strict limits are set by the various governing bodies around the world, and the aim is not to adulterate but to improve the product. Acidity can be adjusted up or down, depending on the climate and alcohol can be increased by adding sugar before fermentation – this is always fermented out so the system cannot legally be used to sweeten wine.

One natural adjustment which has to wait until after the primary alcoholic fermentation is malo-lactic fermentation. Some over-acidic wines contain a high proportion of malic acid, the acid that gives apples their tart flavour. A natural bacterium, called lactobacillus, can be encouraged to break this acid down into lactic, or milk, acid, which is much softer on the palate. This is encouraged with almost all red wines, but only selectively with whites, as many wine makers want to preserve the freshness in the flavour. Malo-lactic fermentation does have another important feature, though. Other chemical components are produced as by-products which have an effect on the taste. The buttery character so often attributed to Chardonnay is often a result of malo-lactic fermentation rather than the grape itself.

Malo-lactic fermentation is, therefore, more than simply an adjustment to the structure, it can be a positive change in the wine's flavour.

Cleaning and bottling

Wine from the vat or barrel is rarely clear, unless it has been maturing for a very long time. Usually it has to be cleaned up before sale. This cleaning takes three forms.

First, the wine maker will chill the wine and hold it at a low temperature to encourage the sedimentation of tartrates. These completely harmless white crystals are a natural part of wine, but they can be off-putting, with many customers mistaking them for sugar crystals or, worse, broken glass in the bottle.

Next, the wine will be fined. There is usually a very fine protein haze in new wine that has to be removed, and filtration will not work. Fining agents include bentonite, a type of earth; egg whites, used in many of the best wines; casein, a milk protein; and isinglass, extracted from fish. It is mainly the fining agents that affect whether or not a wine can be sold as vegetarian or vegan.

The last positive action a wine maker takes before bottling the wine is filtration. This removes any large particles and any remaining yeast and bacteria. White wines with some residual sugar must be filtered, but dry wines, especially those with a high level of alcohol, are more stable and there is an increasing fashion among wine makers to sell their wine unfiltered. This means they are more likely to through with sediment and therefore more likely to need decanting, but filtration takes a little of the body and structure out of the wine. As with everything, a balance has to be struck.

the lore and law of the label

Unless you are buying wine by mail-order, or from a restaurant wine list, your decision will inevitably be influenced by the label. Given the vast range available in any reasonable wine retailer, it will be the general appearance from afar that guides you to pick up one bottle in preference to another. Label design is not an exact science – there is no single correct formula. A wine that to one customer looks boring and old-fashioned is, to another, a sign of reliability and quality; one that is garish to one is lively and trendy to another. The label is the final weapon in the winemakers marketing armoury, it is an advert for itself, but it is also a legal document, guaranteeing that the wine inside the bottle complies with the innumerable rules and regulations governing its production and sale.

In this chapter we will look at some of the terms you will find on the label and explain their meaning and significance to the wine buyer. This cannot be totally comprehensive; some terms mean different things in different countries, or regions, others are invented terms, specific to an individual producer. Oddly, perhaps, the regulations in different importing countries vary too, so that some terms found on Australian wines in the EU would never be seen on the same bottle in the domestic market. Sometimes the laws are so different that mandatory information on, for example, a Californian wine being sold in the San Francisco might be illegal on the same wine sold in London or Paris. We will start with the fundamentals that apply internationally and then look at some of the specifics of European labelling regulations. Finally we will have a look at lot numbering and its uses.

Label integrity

The main reason for labelling laws, wherever the wine comes from, is to ensure that what is claimed on the label is accurate and truthful. If the label says it comes from Chile, then it must, and if it says the Maipo valley in Chile then we have every reason to expect the label to be honest. Wine inspectors in many countries are working on our behalf to ensure fair-play. In the past, when rules were less stringent, wine may not have been what the label claimed. Quite apart from the Spanish Sauternes and Australian Burgundy, both of which sold on price, there were many examples of merchants importing one wine and selling it under different names and labels to suit the market. With the exception of certain generic names still being used in a handful of countries, such as Californian Champagne or Australian Port, we can, today, trust our labels.

Grape varieties on labels

Any claim for a grape variety also has to be honest, but only up to a point. A variety on the label may indicate that the wine is made entirely from that grape, but flexibility exists, allowing a reduction to a minimum, usually of 85%, occasionally 75%. With some grapes, like Riesling, Pinot Noir and Chardonnay, the wine is normally 100% as claimed, but grapes like Cabernet and Merlot benefit from judicious blending with other varieties, either to soften and flesh-out the palate, or to add tannin and structure. Where two or more varieties are quoted they usually make up the entire blend between them, and are listed in descending order of importance, so a Shiraz-Cabernet should have more Shiraz flavour than a Cabernet-Shiraz. It is, incidentally, illegal to over-emphasize a minor component variety, so if a blend contains only 5% Chardonnay, the wine maker cannot list 'Chardonnay' in larger, bolder type than the other grapes.

Wine sold in the European Union has to comply with a whole raft of legislation, one of the more ridiculous requirements being the rule that forbids the inclusion of a grape if not attached to a recognised region. It is, therefore, illegal to have New Zealand Sauvignon Blanc, or Australian Chardonnay without additionally including, say, Marlborough or Barossa. This is a severe restriction on the big, and highly successful branded wines that need to be able to source their fruit from a number of regions. The answer of course has been to create macro regions, following the letter of the law but at the same time highlighting its lunacy. Australia has created the 'South-Eastern Australia' name, an area that covers three states. South Africa has 'Western Cape'. In both cases they potentially cover almost the entire wine production of the country, and in neither case will you see the name on a bottle for sale in the domestic market – these are terms invented purely to get around bureaucracy from Brussels.

The same rule of course applies to wines from within the EU, so a basic table wine (see below) which does not have a region cannot, by extension, state a grape variety.

European Union wine labelling

Europe produces about three-quarters of the world's wines, and the top three producing countries, in terms of volume, are in the European Union so, understandably the EU has some of the most involved rules. To a great extent these are based on the French model, developments of the Appellation Contrôlée (AC, or AOC) system, which after considerable groundwork was finally made law in 1935.

The result is that all wine made in the EU has to fall into one of two broad categories, 'Quality Wine Produced in a Specified Region', or 'Table wine'. Note that table wine therefore has a very specific meaning in the EU now, it is no longer a generic terms for all wine that is not fortified or sparkling.

'Quality Wine Produced in a Specified Region', (QWPSR) deserves some explanation. The word 'Quality' here does not indicate high quality so much as indicating that the wine has certain qualities. In short, the wine has been made in the region stated on the label in accordance with the rules and regulations laid down. These rules will cover the vineyard location, grape varieties used, viticulture, yield, winemaking and maturation, and the wine will have to pass a tasting test to ensure that it is typical of the region. Inevitably there can be a world of difference between two bottles with the same AC, if one has been made with care and attention to detail, and the other just within the law to get the AC.

Another failing of the system is that in many cases, it fails to recognize developments in techniques and fashion. If the wine is made according to the rules, it gets its AC, but those rules rarely change and fashions do. One of the reasons wines from Australia, Chile and California have been so successful is the producers' willingness and ability to develop wines that meet the customer's needs rather than just those of the regulators. Yet originally the rules were promulgated to protect the producers; not the consumers, please note!

'Table wine', on the other hand, was the name given to all other wine. Not made in a famous region, it was assumed that this was going to be poorer in quality and of course cheaper. The rules governing table wine production are more concerned with reducing over production than anything intrinsic about the wine. There are rules governing what can and cannot be included on the labels of the different categories, so that, for example, a simple table wine cannot carry either a grape variety, nor a vintage, and by definition, cannot carry a region. One up from here, table wine with geographical description – Vins de Pays and their equivalents, can carry all three but the region must not be a QWPSR region.

In the last twenty-five years, two distinct developments have been taking place that have changed the face of table wine. First, the creation of Vins de Pays in France. These are wines made outside the AC areas, or at least outside the rules, taking advantage of the flexibility that offers, but still technically humble table wine. The second movement started in Italy, but has since spread to other parts of Europe. Some of the Italian producers saw their laws as too restrictive so, within the QWPSR areas they started to break them. The results were often very fine wines but they were not entitled to be called DOC, or DOCG (see opposite) and carried the most basic Vino da Tavola designation. This led to a change in the law in Italy and to the establishment of an Italian equivalent of Vin de Pays.

Non-EU wines on EU shelves

Wines imported into the EU are officially neither quality wine nor table wine, but simply 'wine' or 'wine with geographical description'. The geographical descriptions have to be acceptable to the EU before they are allowed in and must not cause confusion, for example they must not be able to be confused with a QWPSR region. But including the region on the label does, as we have seen, allow certain advantages, like also including the grape variety. Many countries outside the EU have labelling requirements that directly contradict EU requirements. In the USA, for example, health warnings and additive listing (i.e. 'this wine contains sulfites') is required. Both are not allowed in the EU, so wines from California have to be specially labelled, or have the offending sections covered up by the importer's address.

Lot numbers

In today's litigious world traceably is all important. If a problem comes to light with a wine the bottler needs to be able to recall all the bottles that might be affected, and to do so we have lot numbers. These are mostly for the benefit of the retailer, but there are occasions when the ability to read a lot number is very useful, even for the consumer. They are particularly useful for wines that need to be drunk very young and fresh – in many cases such wines fade after being in the bottle for as little as six months. Fino Sherry is probably the most significant example, but wouldn't it be great to be able to tell how old those apparent bargains are in the bin-ends section of the wine shop?

Well there is good news, and bad news. All wine now has to carry a lot number, unless it is produced in such small quantities that it can all be bottled together and the wine's name and vintage become, in effect, a lot number. All wines can, therefore, be traced and if you are prepared to do some homework you can find out exactly when a particular wine was bottled. The bad news is that there are many different codes used for lot numbers, and many of them are not easily understood. Indeed, some

are very complex alpha-numeric codes that only the producer's computer can decipher – but they hold all manner of information about the wine.

Although there is no one universal standard system, there is one system that is more widely used than others. This is a simple four-figure number that we can all understand. It will appear on the label, sometimes on the capsule or on the bottle itself, preceded by the letter L, so you might see, for example:

L 2345

The first figure is the last digit of the year. We have to take it on trust that, unless it is a wine meant for long ageing, it will be the most recent, so in our example 2002. The other three numbers are the day of the year, counting from 1st January being 001, 2nd being 002 etc, until the 31st December which is 365 (or 366 in leap years). Not information you need everyday, but it can become useful occasionally.

Summary of the main EU terms

France
QWPSR
- Appellation Contrôlée (AC, or AOC) – seen as the top, further subdivided with Grand Crus etc. in certain areas.
- Vin Délimité de Qualité Supérieure, (VDQS) – rarely seen these days, VDQS was meant as a stepping stone to full AC status and most have now been promoted.

Table wines
- Vin de Pays.
- Vin de Table.

Italy
QWPSR
- Denominazione di Orgine Controllata e Ganantita (DOCG) the top grade, established to mark out the very best from the rest of the DOC wines.
- Denominazione di Orgine Controllata (DOC), really the equivalent of the French AC.

Table wines
- Indicazione Geografica Tipica – the Italian equivalent of Vin de Pays.
- Vino da Tavola.

Spain
QWPSR
- Denominación de Origen Calificada (DOC) – the top grade, for Rioja only at the time of writing, equivalent to Italian DOCG.
- Denominación de Origen (DO).

Table wines
- Vino de la Tierra – equivalent to Vin de Pays.
- Vino de Mesa.

Portugal
QWPSR
- Denominação de Origem Controlada (DOC) the AC equivalent.
- Indicacão de Proveniencia Regulamentada (IPR) like VDQS, for wines destined to become DOC. Since the term was created most of the initial IPRs have been promoted.

Table wines
- Vinho Regional.
- Vinho de Mesa.

Germany
- Germany has a different system from the other countries that we have looked at in the chapter on medium and sweet wines.

taking it further

Wine is a fascinating subject that, however diligently you study it, can only remain enjoyable, provided of course that you always remember the dangers of excessive alcohol consumption.

Courses and tastings

It you want to take your studies further and develop your practical tasting skills, you will often find wine appreciation classes are offered at local colleges. These can vary dramatically both in quality and level so do try to speak to the staff and to other participants before you sign up. Some groups are excellent, with well-chosen samples and are accessible to a range of levels of knowledge, but undoubtedly too there are some that are run for the benefit of the tutor's ego.

If a progressive series of courses with formally recognized qualifications appeals, the London-based Wine & Spirit Education Trust (WSET) runs courses at its own offices, and approved centres around the world run courses leading to the (WSET) examinations.

For details contact the WSET on 44 (0)20 7236 3551. Website: www.wset.co.uk.

In some towns and cities the local wine merchant might put on regular tastings. These will usually be one-off tastings, each with its own theme. The aim is to sell wine but don't feel obliged to buy something that is not to your taste.

Books

There are hundreds of books about wine, published worldwide every year, ranging from the all-encompassing encyclopædias to specialist monographs of individual properties. The WSET courses have textbooks that are available separately, and are strongly recommended. Probably the two best general wine references books on the market at the moment are:

The World Atlas of Wine, written by Hugh Johnson and Jancis Robinson, published by Mitchell Beazley (2001).

Oxford Companion to Wine, edited by Jancis Robinson, published by the Oxford University Press (1999).

The WSET® Systematic Approach to Wine Tasting (Intermediate Certificate)

CHECKLIST		EXAMPLES OF TASTING TERMS
APPEARANCE		
Clarity		clear – dull
Intensity		pale – deep
Colour	white	lemon – gold
	rosé	pink – orange
	red	purple - ruby – tawny
NOSE		
Condition		clean – unclean
Intensity		weak – pronounced
Fruit character		e.g.: fruity – floral – vegetal – spicy
PALATE		
Sweetness		dry – sweet
Acidity		low – high
Tannin		low – high
Body		light – full
Fruit character		e.g.: fruity – floral – vegetal – spicy
Length		short – long
CONCLUSIONS		
Quality		poor – acceptable – good

The WSET® Systematic Approach to Wine Tasting (Advanced Certificate)

CHECKLIST	EXAMPLES OF TASTING TERMS
APPEARANCE	

Clarity	clear – dull
Intensity	pale – deep
Colour white	lemon – gold
rosé	pink-orange
red	purple – ruby – tawny
Rim vs core	compare colour and intensity

NOSE	
Condition	clean – unclean
Intensity	weak – pronounced
Development	youthful – aged
Fruit character	e.g.: fruity – floral – vegetal – spicy

PALATE	
Sweetness	dry – medium – sweet
Acidity	low – medium – high
Tannin	low – medium – high
Body	light – medium – full
Fruit intensity	weak – pronounced
Fruit character	e.g.: fruity – floral – vegetal – spicy
Alcohol	light – medium – high
Length	short – medium – long

CONCLUSIONS	
Quality	poor – acceptable – good
Value category	inexpensive – mid-range – premium – super-premium
Maturity	immature – ready to drink

The WSET® Systematic Approach To Wine Tasting (Diploma)

CHECKLIST	EXAMPLES OF TASTING TERMS
APPEARANCE	
Clarity	bright – clear – dull – hazy – cloudy

Intensity   white
            rosé
            red
	water-white – pale – medium – deep
	pale – medium – deep
	pale – medium – deep – opaque

Colour   white
          rosé
          red
	green – lemon – straw – gold – amber – brown
	pink – salmon – orange – onion skin
	purple – ruby – garnet – mahogany – tawny

Other observations	legs, bubbles, rim colour vs core, deposits etc.
NOSE	
Condition	clean – unclean
Intensity	weak – medium – pronounced
Development	youthful/grape aromas – aged bouquet – tired – oxidised (out of condition or deliberate?)
Fruit character	fruity, floral, vegetal, spicy, woods, smoky, animal, mineral (complexity?) fermentation aromas, ripeness, faults
PALATE	
Sweetness	dry – off-dry – medium dry – medium sweet – sweet – luscious
Acidity	flabby – low – balanced – crisp – acidic
Tannin	astringent – hard – balanced – soft
Body	thin – light – medium – full – heavy
Fruit intensity	weak – medium – pronounced
Fruit character	groups as for nose
Alcohol	light – medium – high
Length	short – medium – long
CONCLUSIONS	
Quality (relative to?)	faulty – poor – average – good – outstanding
Maturity	immature (needs x years?) – at peak, can keep (how long?) – at peak, drink soon – declining – over-mature
Age/vintage	[unspecified and partly specified wines]
Origins	location, grape variety/varieties [unspecified wines]
Commercial value	[partly and fully specified wines]

index